Lambert M. Surhone, Miriam T. Timpledon,
Susan F. Marseken (Ed.)

Filter Driver

Lambert M. Surhone, Miriam T. Timpledon,
Susan F. Marseken (Ed.)

Filter Driver

Microsoft Windows, Windows Driver Model, Device Driver

Betascript Publishing

Imprint

Contact:
VDM Publishing House Ltd.,17 Rue Meldrum, Beau Bassin,1713-01 Mauritius
Email: info@vdm-publishing-house.com
Website: www.vdm-publishing-house.com

Published in 2010
Printed in: U.S.A., U.K., Germany. This book was not produced in Mauritius.

ISBN: 978-613-2-22723-2

Contents

Articles

References

Article Licenses

Filter driver

A **filter driver** is a Microsoft Windows driver that adds value to peripheral devices or supports a specialized device in the personal computer. It is a driver/program/module that is inserted into the existing driver stack to perform some specific function. A filter driver should not affect the normal working of the existing driver stack in any major way. Written either by Microsoft or the vendor of the hardware, any number of filter drivers can be added to Windows. Upper level filter drivers sit above the primary driver for the device (the function driver), while lower level filter drivers sit below the function driver and above the bus driver.

Filters may work on a certain brand of device such as a mouse or keyboard, or they may perform some operation on a class of devices, such as any mouse or any keyboard. Another type of filter driver is the bus filter driver, which may be added on top of the bus driver. For example, an ACPI bus filter is added to support power management for each device.

See also

- Windows Driver Model
- Device Driver
- Advanced Configuration and Power Interface

Microsoft Windows

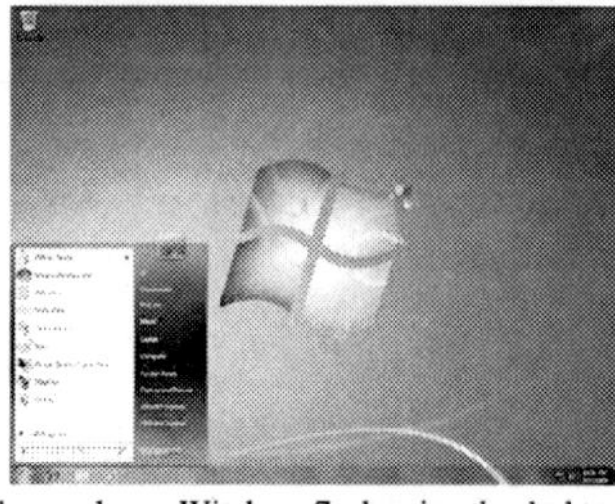

The latest Windows release, Windows 7, showing the desktop and Start menu

Company / developer	Microsoft
Programmed in	C, C++, Assembly[1]
OS family	MS-DOS/Windows 9x-based, Windows CE, Windows NT
Working state	Publicly released
Source model	Closed source / Shared source
Initial release	20 November 1985 (as Windows 1.0)
Latest stable release	[[Windows 7 [2]], Windows Server 2008 R2 NT 6.1 Build 7600 (7600.16385.090713-1255)] (22 October 2009) [3] [+/-]
Latest unstable release	[4] [+/-]
Marketing target	Personal computing
Available language(s)	Multilingual
Update method	Windows Update
Supported platforms	IA-32, x86-64
Kernel type	Hybrid
Default user interface	Graphical (Windows Explorer)
License	MS-EULA
Official website	Official Website [5]

Microsoft Windows is a series of software operating systems and graphical user interfaces produced by Microsoft. Microsoft first introduced an operating environment named *Windows* in November 1985 as an add-on to MS-DOS in response to the growing interest in graphical user interfaces (GUIs).[6] Microsoft Windows came to dominate the world's personal computer market, overtaking Mac OS, which had been introduced previously. As of October 2009, Windows had approximately 91% of the market share of the client operating systems for usage on the Internet.[7] [8] [9] The most recent client version of Windows is Windows 7; the most recent server version is Windows Server 2008 R2; the most recent mobile OS version is Windows Mobile 6.5.

Versions

The term *Windows* collectively describes any or all of several generations of Microsoft operating system products. These products are generally categorized as follows:

Early versions

Windows 1.0, the first version, released in 1985

The history of Windows dates back to September 1981, when the project named "Interface Manager" was started. It was announced in November 1983 (after the Apple Lisa, but before the Macintosh) under the name "Windows", but Windows 1.0 was not released until November 1985.[10] The shell of Windows 1.0 was a program known as the MS-DOS Executive. Other supplied programs were Calculator, Calendar, Cardfile, Clipboard viewer, Clock, Control Panel, Notepad, Paint, Reversi, Terminal, and Write. Windows 1.0 did not allow overlapping windows, due to Apple Computer owning this feature. Instead all windows were tiled. Only dialog boxes could appear over other windows.

Windows 2.0 was released in October 1987 and featured several improvements to the user interface and memory management.[10] Windows 2.0 allowed application windows to overlap each other and also introduced more sophisticated keyboard-shortcuts. It could also make use of expanded memory.

Windows 2.1 was released in two different flavors: Windows/386 employed the 386 virtual 8086 mode to multitask several DOS programs, and the paged memory model to emulate expanded memory using available extended memory. Windows/286 (which, despite its name, would run on the 8086) still ran in real mode, but could make use of the high memory area.

The early versions of Windows were often thought of as simply graphical user interfaces, mostly because they ran on top of MS-DOS and used it for file system services.[11] However, even the earliest 16-bit Windows versions already assumed many typical operating system functions; notably, having their own executable file format and providing their own device drivers (timer, graphics, printer, mouse, keyboard and sound) for applications. Unlike MS-DOS, Windows allowed users to execute multiple graphical applications at the same time, through cooperative multitasking. Windows implemented an elaborate, segment-based, software virtual memory scheme, which allowed it to run applications larger than available memory: code segments and resources were swapped in and thrown away when memory became scarce, and data segments moved in memory when a given application had relinquished processor control, typically waiting for user input.

Windows OS market share

Source	Net Market Share[12]	W3Counter[13]	StatCounter[14]
Date	*May 2010*	*May 2010*	*May 2010*
All versions	91.16%	83.11%	92.32%
Windows XP	62.55%	49.95%	58.02%
Windows Vista	15.25%	17.6%	19.46%
Windows 7	12.68%	14.33%	14.84%
Windows 2000	0.5%	0.34%	—
Windows 98	0.1%	—	—
Windows Me	0.08%	—	—

Windows Server 2003	—	0.89%	—

Windows 3.0 and 3.1

Windows 3.0 (1990) and Windows 3.1 (1992) improved the design, mostly because of virtual memory and loadable virtual device drivers (VxDs) which allowed them to share arbitrary devices between multitasked DOS windows. Also, Windows applications could now run in protected mode (when Windows was running in Standard or 386 Enhanced Mode), which gave them access to several megabytes of memory and removed the obligation to participate in the software virtual memory scheme. They still ran inside the same address space, where the segmented memory provided a degree of protection, and multi-tasked cooperatively. For Windows 3.0, Microsoft also rewrote critical operations from C into assembly, making this release faster and less memory-hungry than its predecessors. With the introduction of Windows for Workgroups 3.11, Windows was able to bypass DOS for file management operations using 32-bit file access.

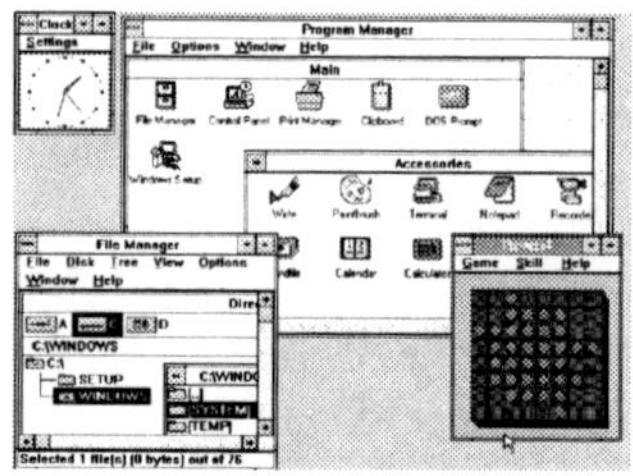

Windows 3.0, released in 1990

Windows 95, 98, and Me

Windows 95 was released in August 1995, featuring a new user interface, support for long file names of up to 255 characters, and the ability to automatically detect and configure installed hardware (plug and play). It could natively run 32-bit applications, and featured several technological improvements that increased its stability over Windows 3.1. There were several OEM Service Releases (OSR) of Windows 95, each of which was roughly equivalent to a service pack.

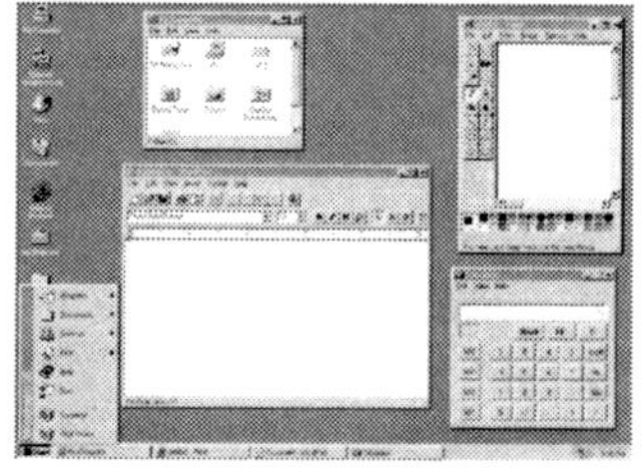

Windows 95, released in 1995

Microsoft's next release was Windows 98 in June 1998. Microsoft released a second version of Windows 98 in May 1999, named Windows 98 Second Edition (often shortened to Windows 98 SE).

In September 2000, Microsoft released Windows Me (*Me* standing for *Millennium Edition*), which updated the core from Windows 98 but adopted some aspects of Windows 2000 and removed the "boot in DOS mode" option. It also added a new feature called System Restore, allowing the user to set the computer's settings back to an earlier date.

Windows NT family

The NT family of Windows systems was fashioned and marketed for higher reliability business use. The first release was NT 3.1 (1993), numbered "3.1" to match the consumer Windows version, which was followed by NT 3.5 (1994), NT 3.51 (1995), NT 4.0 (1996), and Windows 2000 (2000). 2000 is the last NT-based Windows release which does not include Microsoft Product Activation. NT 4.0 was the first in this line to implement the "Windows 95" user interface (and the first to include Windows 95's built-in 32-bit runtimes).

Microsoft then moved to combine their consumer and business operating systems with Windows XP, coming in both home and professional versions (and later niche market versions for tablet PCs and media centers); they also diverged release schedules for server operating systems. Windows Server 2003, released a year and a half after Windows XP, brought Windows Server up to date with MS Windows XP. After a lengthy development process, Windows Vista was released toward the end of 2006, and its server counterpart, Windows Server 2008 was released in early 2008. On July 22, 2009, Windows 7 and Windows Server 2008 R2 were released as RTM (release to manufacturing). Windows 7 was released on October 22, 2009.

64-bit operating systems

Windows NT included support for several different platforms before the x86-based personal computer became dominant in the professional world. Versions of NT from 3.1 to 4.0 variously supported PowerPC, DEC Alpha and MIPS R4000, some of which were 64-bit processors, although the operating system treated them as 32-bit processors.

With the introduction of the Intel Itanium architecture (also known as IA-64), Microsoft released new versions of Windows to support it. Itanium versions of Windows XP and Windows Server 2003 were released at the same time as their mainstream x86 (32-bit) counterparts. On April 25, 2005, Microsoft released Windows XP Professional x64 Edition and Windows Server 2003 x64 Editions to support the x86-64 (or *x64* in Microsoft terminology) architecture. Microsoft dropped support for the Itanium version of Windows XP in 2005. Windows Vista is the first end-user version of Windows that Microsoft has released simultaneously in x86 and x64 editions. Windows Vista does not support the Itanium architecture. The modern 64-bit Windows family comprises AMD64/Intel64 versions of Windows Vista, and Windows Server 2008, in both Itanium and x64 editions. Windows Server 2008 R2 drops the 32-bit version, although Windows 7 does not.

Windows CE

Windows CE (officially known as *Windows Embedded Compact*), is an edition of Windows that runs on minimalistic computers, like satellite navigation systems and some mobile phones. Windows Embedded Compact is based on its own dedicated kernel, dubbed Windows CE kernel. Microsoft licenses Windows CE to OEMs and device makers. The OEMs and device makers can modify and create their own user interfaces and experiences, while Windows CE provides the technical foundation to do so.

The latest upcoming version of Windows CE, Windows Embedded Compact 7, displaying a possible UI for what the media player can look like.

Windows CE was used in the Dreamcast along with Sega's own proprietary OS for the console. Windows CE is the core from which Windows Mobile is derived. Microsoft's latest upcoming version of their mobile OS, Windows Phone 7, is based on components from both Windows CE 6.0 R3 and the upcoming Windows CE 7.0.

Windows Embedded Compact is not to be confused with Windows XP Embedded or Windows NT 4.0 Embedded, modular editions of Windows based on Windows NT kernel.

Future

Windows 8, the successor to Windows 7, is currently in development.

History

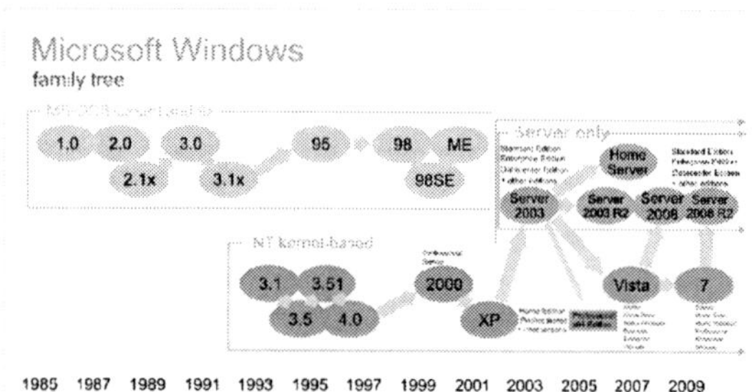

The Windows family tree.

Microsoft has taken two parallel routes in its operating systems. One route has been for the home user and the other has been for the professional IT user. The dual routes have generally led to home versions having greater multimedia support and less functionality in networking and security, and professional versions having inferior multimedia support and better networking and security.

The first version of Microsoft Windows, version 1.0, released in November 1985, lacked a degree of functionality and achieved little popularity, and was to compete with Apple's own operating system. Windows 1.0 is not a complete operating system; rather, it extends MS-DOS. Microsoft Windows version 2.0 was released in November, 1987 and was slightly more popular than its predecessor. Windows 2.03 (release date January 1988) had changed the OS from tiled windows to overlapping windows. The result of this change led to Apple Computer filing a suit against Microsoft alleging infringement on Apple's copyrights.[15] [16]

Microsoft Windows 3.0, released in 1990, was the first Microsoft Windows version to achieve broad commercial success, selling 2 million copies in the first six months.[17] [18] It featured improvements to the user interface and to multitasking capabilities. It received a facelift in Windows 3.1, made generally available on March 1, 1992. Windows 3.1 support ended on December 31, 2001.[19]

In July 1993, Microsoft released Windows NT based on a new kernel. NT was considered to be the professional OS and was the first Windows version to utilize preemptive multitasking.. Windows NT would later be retooled to also function as a home operating system, with Windows XP.

On August 24, 1995, Microsoft released Windows 95, a new, and major, consumer version that made further changes to the user interface, and also used preemptive multitasking. Windows 95 was designed to replace not only Windows 3.1, but also Windows for Workgroups, and MS-DOS. It was also the first Windows operating system to use Plug and Play capabilities. The changes Windows 95 brought to the desktop were revolutionary, as opposed to evolutionary, such as those in Windows 98 and Windows Me. Mainstream support for Windows 95 ended on December 31, 2000 and extended support for Windows 95 ended on December 31, 2001.[20]

The next in the consumer line was Microsoft Windows 98 released on June 25, 1998. It was substantially criticized for its slowness and for its unreliability compared with Windows 95, but many of its basic problems were later rectified with the release of Windows 98 Second Edition (98SE) in 1999. Mainstream support for Windows 98 ended on June 30, 2002 and extended support for Windows 98 ended on July 11, 2006.[21]

As part of its "professional" line, Microsoft released Windows 2000 in February 2000. During 2004 part of the Source Code for Windows 2000 was leaked onto the internet. This was bad for Microsoft as the same kernel used in Windows 2000 was used in Windows XP. The consumer version following Windows 98 was Windows Me (Windows Millennium Edition). Released in September 2000, Windows Me implemented a number of new technologies for Microsoft: most notably publicized was "Universal Plug and Play". Windows Me was criticized a lot, due to slownesses, freezes and hardware problems.

In October 2001, Microsoft released Windows XP, a version built on the Windows NT kernel that also retained the consumer-oriented usability of Windows 95 and its successors. This new version was widely praised in computer magazines.[22] It shipped in two distinct editions, "Home" and "Professional", the former lacking many of the superior security and networking features of the Professional edition. Additionally, the first "Media Center" edition was released in 2002,[23] with an emphasis on support for DVD and TV functionality including program recording and a remote control. Mainstream support for Windows XP ended on April 14, 2009. Extended support will continue until April 8, 2014.[24]

In April 2003, Windows Server 2003 was introduced, replacing the Windows 2000 line of server products with a number of new features and a strong focus on security; this was followed in December 2005 by Windows Server 2003 R2.

On January 30, 2007 Microsoft released Windows Vista. It contains a number of new features, from a redesigned shell and user interface to significant technical changes, with a particular focus on security features. It is available in a number of different editions, and has been subject to some criticism.

Timeline of releases

Timeline of releases				
Release date	**Product name**	**Current Version / Build**	**Notes**	**Last IE**
November 1985	Windows 1.01	1.01	Unsupported	-
November 1987	Windows 2.03	2.03	Unsupported	-
May 1988	Windows 2.10	2.10	Unsupported	-
March 1989	Windows 2.11	2.11	Unsupported	-
May 1990	Windows 3.0	3.0	Unsupported	-
March 1992	Windows 3.1x	3.1	Unsupported	5
October 1992	Windows For Workgroups 3.1	3.1	Unsupported	5
July 1993	Windows NT 3.1	NT 3.1	Unsupported	5
December 1993	Windows For Workgroups 3.11	3.11	Unsupported	5
January 1994	Windows 3.2 (released in Simplified Chinese only)	3.2	Unsupported	5
September 1994	Windows NT 3.5	NT 3.5	Unsupported	5
May 1995	Windows NT 3.51	NT 3.51	Unsupported	5
August 1995	Windows 95	4.0.950	Unsupported[25]	5.5
July 1996	Windows NT 4.0	NT 4.0.1381	Unsupported[26]	6
June 1998	Windows 98	4.10.1998	Unsupported[27]	6
May 1999	Windows 98 SE	4.10.2222	Unsupported[28]	6
February 2000	Windows 2000	NT 5.0.2195	Unsupported[29]	6
September 2000	Windows Me	4.90.3000	Unsupported[30]	6

October 2001	Windows XP	NT 5.1.2600	Extended Support until April 8, 2014 for SP3. (RTM, SP1 and SP2 unsupported).	8
March 2003	Windows XP 64-bit Edition (IA-64)	NT 5.2.3790	Unsupported	6
April 2003	Windows Server 2003	NT 5.2.3790	Current (RTM and SP1 unsupported)	8
April 2005	Windows XP Professional x64 Edition	NT 5.2.3790	Extended Support for SP2 until April 8, 2014. (RTM and SP1 unsupported).	8
July 2006	Windows Fundamentals for Legacy PCs	NT 5.1.2600	Current	8
November 2006 (volume licensing) January 2007 (retail)	Windows Vista	NT 6.0.6002	Current (RTM unsupported). Version changed to NT 6.0.6001 with SP1 (February 4, 2008) and to NT 6.0.6002 with SP2 (April 28, 2009).	9
July 2007	Windows Home Server	NT 5.2.4500	Current	8
February 2008	Windows Server 2008	NT 6.0.6002	Current Version changed to NT 6.0.6002 with SP2 (April 28, 2009).	9
October 2009 [31]	Windows 7 and Windows Server 2008 R2	NT 6.1.7600	Current	9

Security

Consumer versions of Windows were originally designed for ease-of-use on a single-user PC without a network connection, and did not have security features built in from the outset.[32] However, Windows NT and its successors are designed for security (including on a network) and multi-user PCs, but were not initially designed with Internet security in mind as much, since, when it was first developed in the early 1990s, Internet use was less prevalent.[33]

These design issues combined with programming errors (e.g. buffer overflows) and the popularity of Windows means that it is a frequent target of computer worm and virus writers. In June 2005, Bruce Schneier's *Counterpane Internet Security* reported that it had seen over 1,000 new viruses and worms in the previous six months.[34]

Microsoft releases security patches through its Windows Update service approximately once a month (usually the second Tuesday of the month), although critical updates are made available at shorter intervals when necessary.[35] In versions of Windows after and including Windows 2000 SP3 and Windows XP, updates can be automatically downloaded and installed if the user selects to do so. As a result, Service Pack 2 for Windows XP, as well as Service Pack 1 for Windows Server 2003, were installed by users more quickly than it otherwise might have been.[36]

While the Windows 9x series offered the option of having profiles for multiple users, they had no concept of access privileges, and did not allow concurrent access; and so were not true multi-user operating systems. In addition, they implemented only partial memory protection. They were accordingly widely criticised for lack of security.

The Windows NT series of operating systems, by contrast, are true multi-user, and implement absolute memory protection. However, a lot of the advantages of being a true multi-user operating system were nullified by the fact that, prior to Windows Vista, the first user account created during the setup process was an administrator account, which was also the default for new accounts. Though Windows XP did have limited accounts, the majority of home users did not change to an account type with fewer rights – partially due to the number of programs which unnecessarily required administrator rights – and so most home users ran as administrator all the time.

Windows Vista changes this[37] by introducing a privilege elevation system called User Account Control. When logging in as a standard user, a logon session is created and a token containing only the most basic privileges is assigned. In this way, the new logon session is incapable of making changes that would affect the entire system.

When logging in as a user in the Administrators group, two separate tokens are assigned. The first token contains all privileges typically awarded to an administrator, and the second is a restricted token similar to what a standard user would receive. User applications, including the Windows Shell, are then started with the restricted token, resulting in a reduced privilege environment even under an Administrator account. When an application requests higher privileges or "Run as administrator" is clicked, UAC will prompt for confirmation and, if consent is given (including administrator credentials if the account requesting the elevation is not a member of the administrators group), start the process using the unrestricted token.[38]

File permissions

All Windows versions from Windows NT 3 have been based on a file system permission system referred to as AGLP (Accounts, Global, Local, Permissions) AGDLP which in essence where file permissions are applied to the file/folder in the form of a 'local group' which then has other 'global groups' as members. These global groups then hold other groups or users depending on different Windows versions used. This system varies from other vendor products such as Linux and NetWare due to the 'static' allocation of permission being applied directory to the file or folder. However using this process of AGLP/AGDLP/AGUDLP allows a small number of static permissions to be applied and allows for easy changes to the account groups without reapplying the file permissions on the files and folders.

Windows Defender

On January 6, 2005, Microsoft released a Beta version of Microsoft AntiSpyware, based upon the previously released Giant AntiSpyware. On February 14, 2006, Microsoft AntiSpyware became Windows Defender with the release of Beta 2. Windows Defender is a freeware program designed to protect against spyware and other unwanted software. Windows XP and Windows Server 2003 users who have genuine copies of Microsoft Windows can freely download the program from Microsoft's web site, and Windows Defender ships as part of Windows Vista and 7.[39]

Third-party analysis

In an article based on a report by Symantec,[40] internetnews.com has described Microsoft Windows as having the "fewest number of patches and the shortest average patch development time of the five operating systems it monitored in the last six months of 2006."[41]

A study conducted by Kevin Mitnick and marketing communications firm Avantgarde in 2004 found that an unprotected and unpatched Windows XP system with Service Pack 1 lasted only 4 minutes on the Internet before it was compromised, and an unprotected and also unpatched Windows Server 2003 system was compromised after being connected to the internet for 8 hours.[42] However, it is important to note that this study does not apply to Windows XP systems running the Service Pack 2 update (released in late 2004), which vastly improved the security of Windows XP. The computer that was running Windows XP Service Pack 2 was not compromised. The AOL National Cyber Security Alliance Online Safety Study of October 2004 determined that 80% of Windows users were infected by at least one spyware/adware product.[43] Much documentation is available describing how to increase the security of Microsoft Windows products. Typical suggestions include deploying Microsoft Windows behind a hardware or software firewall, running anti-virus and anti-spyware software, and installing patches as they become available through Windows Update.[44]

Emulation software

Emulation allows the use of some Windows applications without using Microsoft Windows. These include:

- Wine — a free and open source software implementation of the Windows API, allowing one to run many Windows applications on x86-based platforms, including Linux and Mac OS X. Wine developers refer to it as a "compatibility layer";[45] and make use of Windows-style APIs to emulate the Windows environment.
  - CrossOver — A Wine package with licensed fonts. Its developers are regular contributors to Wine, and focus on Wine running officially supported applications.
  - Cedega — TransGaming Technologies' proprietary fork of Wine, designed specifically for running games written for Microsoft Windows under Linux. A version of Cedega known as Cider is used by some video game publishers to allow Windows games to run on Mac OS X. Since wine was licensed under the LGPL Cedega has been unable to port the improvements made to wine to their proprietary codebase.
  - Darwine — A bundling of Wine to the PowerPC Macs running OS X by running wine on top of QEMU. Intel Macs use the same Wine as other *NIX x86 systems.
- ReactOS — An open-source OS that is intended to run the same software as Windows, originally designed to simulate Windows NT 4.0, now aiming at Windows XP and Vista/7 compatibility. It has been in the development stage since 1996.

See also

General:

- Architecture of the Windows NT operating system line
- List of Microsoft Windows components
- Criticism of Microsoft Windows
- Comparison of operating systems
- Comparison of Windows and Linux
- Comparison of Windows versions
- List of operating systems
- Market share of operating systems
- Wintel

External links

- Official Microsoft Windows Website [46]
- Microsoft Developer Network [47]
- Microsoft Windows History Timeline [48]
- Pearson Education, InformIT [49] – History of Microsoft Windows

References

[1] Microsoft Windows System Overview (http://www.microsoft.com/technet/archive/winntas/training/ntarchitectoview/ntarc_2.mspx)

[2] http://en.wikipedia.org/wiki/Template%3Alatest_stable_software_release%2Fwindows_nt

[3] http://en.wikipedia.org/wiki/Template%3Alatest_stable_software_release%2Fmicrosoft_windows

[4] http://en.wikipedia.org/wiki/Template%3Alatest_preview_software_release%2Fmicrosoft_windows

[5] http://www.microsoft.com/windows/

[6] "The Unusual History of Microsoft Windows" (http://inventors.about.com/od/mstartinventions/a/Windows.htm?rd=1). . Retrieved 2007-04-22.

[7] "Global Web Stats" (http://www.w3counter.com/globalstats.php). W3Counter, Awio Web Services. September 2009. . Retrieved 2009-10-24.

[8] "Operating System Market Share" (http://marketshare.hitslink.com/operating-system-market-share.aspx?qprid=8). Net Applications. October 2009. . Retrieved November 5, 2009.

[9] "Top 5 Operating Systems on Oct 09" (http://gs.statcounter.com/#os-ww-monthly-200910-200910-bar). StatCounter. October 2009. . Retrieved November 5, 2009.
[10] Petzold
[11] "Windows Evolution" (http://news.soft32.com/windows-evolution_1629.html). Soft32.com News. .
[12] "Net Applications Operating System Market Share" (http://marketshare.hitslink.com/operating-system-market-share.aspx?qprid=10&qpcal=1&qpcal=1&qpcal=1&qptimeframe=M&qpsp=136). Net Market Share. May 2010. .
[13] "Global Web Stats" (http://w3counter.com/globalstats.php?year=2010&month=5). W3Counter. May 2010. .
[14] "StatCounter Global Stats" (http://gs.statcounter.com/#os-ww-monthly-201005-201005-bar). StatCounter. May 2010. .
[15] "The Apple vs. Microsoft GUI Lawsuit" (http://lowendmac.com/orchard/06/apple-vs-microsoft.html). 2006. . Retrieved 2008-03-12
[16] "Apple Computer, Inc. v. MicroSoft Corp., 35 F.3d 1435 (9th Cir. 1994)" (http://home.earthlink.net/~mjohnsen/Technology/Lawsuits/appvsms.html). . Retrieved 2008-03-12
[17] "Chronology of Personal Computer Software" (http://www.islandnet.com/~kpolsson/compsoft/soft1991.htm). .
[18] "Microsoft Company" (http://www.thocp.net/companies/microsoft/microsoft_company.htm). .
[19] Windows 3.1 Standard Edition Support Lifecycle (http://support.microsoft.com/lifecycle/?p1=3078)
[20] Windows 95 Support Lifecycle (http://support.microsoft.com/lifecycle/?p1=7864)
[21] Windows 98 Standard Edition Support Lifecycle (http://support.microsoft.com/lifecycle/?p1=6513)
[22] Your top Windows XP questions answered! (Part One) (http://web.archive.org/web/20071219121319/http://review.zdnet.com/4520-6033_16-4206367.html)
[23] Paul Thurrott's SuperSite for Windows: A Look at Freestyle and Mira (http://www.winsupersite.com/showcase/freestyle_preview.asp)
[24] Windows XP Professional Lifecycle Support (http://support.microsoft.com/lifecycle/?p1=3223)
[25] "Windows 95 Support Lifecycle" (http://support.microsoft.com/lifecycle/?p1=7864). Microsoft. 2001. . Retrieved 2010-07-14.
[26] "Windows NT Embedded 4.0 Support Lifecycle" (http://support.microsoft.com/lifecycle/?p1=3185). Microsoft. 2005. . Retrieved 2010-07-14.
[27] "Windows 98 Standard Edition Support Lifecycle" (http://support.microsoft.com/lifecycle/?p1=6513). Microsoft. 2006. . Retrieved 2010-07-14.
[28] "Windows 98 Second Edition Support Lifecycle" (http://support.microsoft.com/lifecycle/?p1=6898). Microsoft. 2006. . Retrieved 2010-07-14.
[29] "Windows 2000 Professional Edition Support Lifecycle" (http://support.microsoft.com/lifecycle/?p1=3071). Microsoft. May 4, 2005. . Retrieved 2007-03-25.
[30] "Windows 98 Second Edition Support Lifecycle" (http://support.microsoft.com/lifecycle/?p1=6519). Microsoft. 2006. . Retrieved 2010-07-14.
[31] "Microsoft Delivers New Wave of Technologies to Help Businesses Thrive in Today's Economy" (http://www.microsoft.com/presspass/press/2009/May09/05-11TechEd09PR.mspx?rss_fdn=Press Releases). Microsoft. 2009-05-11. . Retrieved 2009-05-22.
[32] Multi-user memory protection was not introduced until Windows NT and XP, and a computer's default user was an administrator until Windows Vista. Source: UAC msdn (http://blogs.msdn.com/uac/)
[33] "Telephones and Internet Users by Country, 1990 and 2005" (http://www.infoplease.com/ipa/A0883396.html). Information Please Database. . Retrieved 2009-06-09.
[34] Schneier, Bruce (2005-06-15). "Crypto-Gram Newsletter" (http://www.schneier.com/crypto-gram-0506.html). Counterpane Internet Security, Inc.. . Retrieved 2007-04-22.
[35] Naraine, Ryan (2005-06-08). "Microsoft's Security Response Center: How Little Patches Are Made" (http://www.eweek.com/c/a/Windows/Microsofts-Security-Response-Center-How-Little-Patches-Are-Made/). eWeek. . Retrieved 2007-04-22.
[36] Foley, John (2004-10-20). "Windows XP SP2 Distribution Surpasses 100 Million" (http://www.informationweek.com/news/security/vulnerabilities/showArticle.jhtml?articleID=50900297). InformationWeek. . Retrieved 2007-04-22.
[37] Microsoft describes in detail the steps taken to combat this in a TechNet bulletin. (http://technet.microsoft.com/en-us/windowsvista/aa905073.aspx)
[38] Kenny Kerr (2006-09-29). "Windows Vista for Developers – Part 4 – User Account Control" (http://weblogs.asp.net/kennykerr/archive/2006/09/29/Windows-Vista-for-Developers-_1320_-Part-4-_1320_-User-Account-Control.aspx). . Retrieved 2007-03-15.
[39] "Windows Vista: Features" (http://www.Microsoft.com/Windowsvista/features/foreveryone/security.mspx). MicroSoft. . Retrieved 2006-07-20.
[40] "Symantec 11th Internet Security Threat Report, Trends for July–December 6" (http://www.symantec.com/business/theme.jsp?themeid=threatreport). .
[41] "Report Says Windows Gets The Fastest Repairs" (http://www.internetnews.com/security/article.php/3667201). .
[42] "Automated "Bots" Overtake PCs Without Firewalls Within 4 Minutes" (http://www.avantgarde.com/ttln113004.html). Avant Garde. .
[43] "Safety Study" (http://web.archive.org/web/20051102045804/http://www.staysafeonline.info/pdf/safety_study_v04.pdf) (PDF). Stay Safe Online. Archived from the original (http://www.staysafeonline.info/pdf/safety_study_v04.pdf) on 2005-11-02. .
[44] 5 Steps to Securing Your Windows XP Home Computer (http://www.computer-security-news.com/0969/5-steps-to-securing-your-windows-xp-home-computer)
[45] "Wine" (http://www.winehq.org/). .
[46] http://www.microsoft.com/Windows/

[47] http://www.msdn.com/
[48] http://www.microsoft.com/Windows/WinHistoryIntro.mspx
[49] http://www.informit.com/articles/article.aspx?p=1358665&rll=1

Windows Driver Model

In computing, the **Windows Driver Model (WDM)** — also known at one point as the **Win32 Driver Model** — is a framework for device drivers that was introduced with Windows 98 and Windows 2000 to replace VxD, which was used on older versions of Windows such as Windows 95 and Windows 3.1, as well as the Windows NT Driver Model.

Overview

WDM drivers are layered in a complex hierarchy and communicate with each other via I/O request packets (IRPs). The Microsoft Windows Driver Model defined a unified driver model for the Windows 98 and Windows 2000 lines by standardizing requirements and reducing the amount of code that needed to be written. WDM drivers will not run on operating systems earlier than Windows 98 or Windows 2000, such as Windows 95, Windows NT 4.0 and Windows 3.1. By conforming to WDM, drivers can be binary compatible and source-compatible across Windows 98, Windows 98 Second Edition, Windows Me, Windows 2000, Windows XP, Windows Server 2003 and Windows Vista (for backwards compatibility) on x86-based computers. WDM drivers are designed to be forward-compatible so that a WDM driver can run on a version of Windows newer than what the driver was initially written for, but doing that would mean that the driver cannot take advantage of any new features introduced with the new version. WDM is generally not backward-compatible, that is, a WDM driver is not guaranteed to run on any older version of Windows. For example, Windows XP can use a driver written for Windows 2000 but will not make use of any of the new WDM features that were introduced in Windows XP. However, a driver written for Windows XP may or may not load on Windows 2000.

WDM exists in the intermediary layer of Windows 2000 kernel-mode drivers and was introduced to increase the functionality and ease of writing drivers for Windows. Although WDM was mainly designed to be binary and source compatible between Windows 98 and Windows 2000, this may not always be desired and so specific drivers can be developed for either operating system. WDM drivers can be classified into the following types and sub-types:

Device function drivers

A **function driver** is the main driver for a device. A function driver is typically written by the device vendor and is required (unless the device is being used in raw mode). A function driver can service one or more devices.

- **Class drivers:** These are a type of *function drivers* and can be thought of as built-in *framework* drivers that miniport and other class drivers can be built on top of. The class drivers provide interfaces between different levels of the WDM architecture. Common functionality between different classes of drivers can be written into the class driver and used by other class and miniport drivers. The lower edge of the class driver will have its interface exposed to the miniport driver, while the upper edge of top level class drivers is operating system specific. Class drivers can be dynamically loaded and unloaded at will. They can do class specific functions that are not hardware or bus-specific (with the exception of bus-type class drivers) and in fact sometimes only do class specific functions like enumeration.
- **Miniport drivers:** These are also *function drivers* for USB, Audio, SCSI and network adapters. They should usually be source and binary compatible between Windows 98 and Windows 2000 and are hardware specific but control access to the hardware through a specific bus class driver.

Bus drivers

A **bus driver** services a bus controller, adapter, or bridge. Microsoft provides bus drivers for most common buses, such as PCI, PnPISA, SCSI, USB and FireWire. Each software vendor can create their own bus drivers if needed. A bus driver can service more than one bus if there is more than one bus of the same type on the machine.

Filter drivers

Filter drivers are optional drivers that add value to or modify the behavior of a device and may be non-device drivers. A filter driver can also service one or more devices. Upper level filter drivers sit above the primary driver for the device (the function driver), while lower level filter drivers sit below the function driver and above the bus driver.

- **Driver service:** This is a type of kernel-level filter driver implemented as a Windows service that enables applications to work with devices.

VxD, WDM and Windows 98

Windows 98 based operating systems (Windows 98, Windows 98 Second Edition, and Windows Me) are able to use both WDM and VxD (Virtual device driver) driver standards. Both drivers models can provide unique and different features for the same hardware. However, usually the newer WDM standard provides more features. For example, if a TV tuner card using a VxD driver is able to capture images at a resolution of 384 x 288 pixels, the same TV Tuner card with the WDM driver model may be able to capture at a resolution of 768 x 576 pixels. This can be attributed to the new Broadcast Driver Architecture model which is part of WDM.

Criticism

The Windows Driver Model, while a significant improvement over the VxD and Windows NT driver model used before it, has been criticised by driver software developers [1], most significantly for the following:

- WDM has a very shallow learning curve.
- Interactions with power management events and plug and play are difficult. This leads to a variety of situations where Windows machines cannot go to sleep or wake up correctly due to bugs in driver code.
- I/O cancellation is almost impossible to get right.
- Thousands of lines of support code are required for every driver.
- No support for writing pure user-mode drivers.

There were also a number of concerns about the quality of documentation and samples that Microsoft provided.

Because of these issues, Microsoft has released a new framework to replace WDM, called the Windows Driver Foundation, which includes Kernel-Mode Driver Framework (KMDF) and User-Mode Driver Framework (UMDF). Windows Vista supports both WDM and the newer Windows Driver Foundation. KMDF is also available for download for Windows XP and even Windows 2000, while UMDF is available for Windows XP.

See also

- Windows Driver Foundation
- Kernel-Mode Driver Framework
- User-Mode Driver Framework
  - Windows Display Driver Model

References

- Finnel, Lynn (2000). *MCSE Exam 70-215, Microsoft Windows 2000 Server*. Microsoft Press. ISBN 1-57231-903-8.
- Oney, Walter (2003). *Programming the Windows Driver Model*, Microsoft Press, ISBN 0-7356-1803-8.

External links

- Windows driver API basics [2] - This article informs you about the basics behind soundcard drivers such as WDM, ASIO, MME, DirectX, etc.
- Channel 9 Video [3] - Interview with the Device Management and Installation team at Microsoft, primarily covering Plug-and-play.
- Kernel Survival guide [4] - Free lecture notes book fragment detailing basic creation of Windows Drivers, Kernel Mode programming, and Memory management

References

[1] http://www.wd-3.com/archive/FrameworkIntro.htm
[2] http://www.staudio.de/kb/english/drivers/
[3] http://channel9.msdn.com/Showpost.aspx?postid=156316
[4] http://hisown.com/Talks/WK.pdf

Device Driver

In computing, a **device driver** or **software driver** is a computer program allowing higher-level computer programs to interact with a hardware device.

A driver typically communicates with the device through the computer bus or communications subsystem to which the hardware connects. When a calling program invokes a routine in the driver, the driver issues commands to the device. Once the device sends data back to the driver, the driver may invoke routines in the original calling program. Drivers are hardware-dependent and operating-system-specific. They usually provide the interrupt handling required for any necessary asynchronous time-dependent hardware interface.

Purpose

A device driver simplifies programming by acting as a translator between a hardware device and the applications or operating systems that use it. Programmers can write the higher-level application code independently of whatever specific hardware device it will ultimately control, because code and device can interface in a standard way, regardless of the software superstructure or of underlying hardware. Every version of a device, such as a printer, requires its own hardware-specific specialized commands. In contrast, most applications utilize devices (such as a file to a printer) by means of high-level device-generic commands such as PRINTLN (print a line). The device-driver accepts these generic high-level commands and breaks them into a series of low-level device-specific commands as required by the device being driven. Furthermore, drivers can provide a level of security as they can run in kernel-mode, thereby protecting the operating system from applications running in user-mode.

Design

Device drivers can be abstracted into logical and physical layers. Logical layers process data for a class of devices such as Ethernet ports or disk drives. Physical layers communicate with specific device instances. For example, a serial port needs to handle standard communication protocols such as XON/XOFF that are common for all serial port hardware. This would be managed by a serial port logical layer. However, the physical layer needs to communicate with a particular serial port chip. 16550 UART hardware differs from PL-011. The physical layer addresses these chip-specific variations. Conventionally, OS requests go to the logical layer first. In turn, the logical layer calls upon the physical layer to implement OS requests in terms understandable by the hardware. Inversely, when a hardware device needs to respond to the OS, it uses the physical layer to speak to the logical layer.

In Linux environments, programmers can build device drivers either as parts of the kernel or separately as loadable modules. Makedev includes a list of the devices in Linux: ttyS (terminal), lp (parallel port), hd (disk), loop (loopback disk device), sound (these include mixer, sequencer, dsp, and audio)... [1]

The Microsoft Windows .sys files and Linux .ko modules contain loadable device drivers. The advantage of loadable device drivers is that they can be loaded only when necessary and then unloaded, thus saving kernel memory.

Development

Writing a device driver requires an in-depth understanding of how the hardware and the software of a given platform function. Drivers operate in a highly privileged environment and can cause disaster if they get things wrong.[2] In contrast, most user-level software on modern operating systems can be stopped without greatly affecting the rest of the system. Even drivers executing in user mode can crash a system if the device is erroneously programmed. These factors make it more difficult and dangerous to diagnose problems.

Thus the task of writing drivers usually falls to software engineers who work for hardware-development companies. This is because they have better information than most outsiders about the design of their hardware. Moreover, it was traditionally considered in the hardware manufacturer's interest to guarantee that their clients can use their hardware in an optimum way. Typically, the *logical device driver* (LDD) is written by the operating system vendor, while the *physical device driver* (PDD) is implemented by the device vendor. But in recent years non-vendors have written numerous device drivers, mainly for use with free and open source operating systems. In such cases, it is important that the hardware manufacturer provides information on how the device communicates. Although this information can instead be learned by reverse engineering, this is much more difficult with hardware than it is with software.

Microsoft has attempted to reduce system instability due to poorly written device drivers by creating a new framework for driver development, called Windows Driver Foundation (WDF). This includes User-Mode Driver Framework (UMDF) that encourages development of certain types of drivers — primarily those that implement a message-based protocol for communicating with their devices — as user mode drivers. If such drivers malfunction, they do not cause system instability. The Kernel-Mode Driver Framework (KMDF) model continues to allow development of kernel-mode device drivers, but attempts to provide standard implementations of functions that are well known to cause problems, including cancellation of I/O operations, power management, and plug and play device support.

Apple has an open-source framework for developing drivers on Mac OS X called the I/O Kit.

Kernel-mode vs user-mode

Device drivers, particularly on modern Windows platforms, can run in kernel-mode (Ring 0) or in user-mode (Ring 3).[3] The primary benefit of running a driver in user mode is improved stability, since a poorly written user mode device driver cannot crash the system by overwriting kernel memory.[4] On the other hand, user/kernel-mode transitions usually impose a considerable performance overhead, thereby prohibiting user mode-drivers for low latency and high throughput requirements.

Kernel space can be accessed by user module only through the use of system calls. End user programs like the UNIX shell or other GUI based applications are part of the user space. These applications interact with hardware through kernel supported functions.

Applications

Because of the diversity of modern hardware and operating systems, drivers operate in many different environments. Drivers may interface with:

- printers
- video adapters
- network cards
- Sound cards
- local buses of various sorts — in particular, for bus mastering on modern systems
- low-bandwidth I/O buses of various sorts (for pointing devices such as mice, keyboards, USB, etc.)
- computer storage devices such as hard disk, CD-ROM and floppy disk buses (ATA, SATA, SCSI)
- implementing support for different file systems
- image scanners
- digital cameras

Common levels of abstraction for device drivers include:

- for hardware:
  - interfacing directly
  - writing to or reading from a device control register
  - using some higher-level interface (e.g. Video BIOS)

- using another lower-level device driver (e.g. file system drivers using disk drivers)
- simulating work with hardware, while doing something entirely different
- for software:
  - allowing the operating system direct access to hardware resources
  - implementing only primitives
  - implementing an interface for non-driver software (e.g. TWAIN)
  - implementing a language, sometimes quite high-level (e.g. PostScript)

Choosing and installing the correct device drivers for given hardware is often a key component of computer system configuration.

Virtual device drivers

Virtual device drivers represent a particular variant of device drivers. They are used to emulate a hardware device, particularly in virtualization environments, for example when a DOS program is run on a Microsoft Windows computer or when a guest operating system is run on, for example, a Xen host. Instead of enabling the guest operating system to dialog with hardware, virtual device drivers take the opposite role and emulate a piece of hardware, so that the guest operating system and its drivers running inside a virtual machine can have the illusion of accessing real hardware. Attempts by the guest operating system to access the hardware are routed to the virtual device driver in the host operating system as e.g. function calls. The virtual device driver can also send simulated processor-level events like interrupts into the virtual machine.

Virtual devices may also operate in a non-virtualized environment. For example a virtual network adapter is used with a virtual private network, while a virtual disk device is used with iSCSI.

Open drivers

- Printers: CUPS
- Scanners: SANE
- Video: Vidix, Direct Rendering Infrastructure

Solaris descriptions of commonly-used device drivers

- fas: Fast/wide SCSI controller
- hme: Fast (10/100 Mbit/s) Ethernet
- isp: Differential SCSI controllers and the SunSwift card
- glm: (Gigabaud Link Module[5]) UltraSCSI controllers
- scsi: Small Computer Serial Interface (SCSI) devices
- sf: soc+ or socal Fiber Channel Arbitrated Loop (FCAL)
- soc: SPARC Storage Array (SSA) controllers
- socal: Serial optical controllers for FCAL (soc+)

APIs

- Advanced Linux Sound Architecture (ALSA) - as of 2009 the standard Linux sound-driver interface
- I/O Kit - an open-source framework from Apple for developing Mac OS X device drivers
- Installable File System (IFS) - a filesystem API for IBM OS/2 and Microsoft Windows NT
- Network Driver Interface Specification (NDIS) - a standard network card driver API
- Open Data-Link Interface (ODI) - a network card API similar to NDIS
- Scanner Access Now Easy (SANE) - a public-domain interface to raster-image scanner-hardware
- Uniform Driver Interface (UDI) - a cross-platform driver interface project
- Windows Display Driver Model (WDDM) - the graphic display driver architecture for Windows Vista
- Windows Driver Foundation (WDF)
- Windows Driver Model (WDM)

Identifiers

- Device id is the device identifier and Vendor id is the vendor identifier.

See also

- Class driver
- Firmware
- Interrupt
- Loadable kernel module
- Makedev
- Open-source hardware
- Printer driver
- udev

External links

- Microsoft Windows Hardware Developer Central [6]
- Linux Hardware Compatibility Lists and Linux Drivers [7]
- Writing Device Drivers: A Tutorial [8]
- If you wish to have Linux drivers written for your device [9]
- Free Linux Driver Development Questions and Answers [10]
- Linux hardware [11]
- O'Reilly e-book: Linux Device Drivers, Third Edition [12]

zs:驱动程序

References

[1] "MAKEDEV — Linux Command — Unix Command" (http://linux.about.com/od/commands/l/blcmdl8_MAKEDEV.htm). Linux.about.com. 2009-09-11. . Retrieved 2009-09-17.
[2] "Device Driver Basics" (http://www.linux-tutorial.info/modules.php?name=Tutorial&pageid=255). .
[3] "User-mode vs. Kernel-mode Drivers" (http://technet2.microsoft.com/windowsserver/en/library/eb1936c0-e19c-4a17-a1a8-39292e4929a41033.mspx?mfr=true). Microsoft. 2003-03-01. . Retrieved 2008-03-04.
[4] "Introduction to the User-Mode Driver Framework (UMDF)" (http://blogs.msdn.com/iliast/archive/2006/10/10/Introduction-to-the-User_2D00_Mode-Driver-Framework.aspx). Microsoft. 2006-10-10. . Retrieved 2008-03-04.
[5] "US Patent 5969841 - Gigabaud link module with received power detect signal" (http://www.patentstorm.us/patents/5969841.html). PatentStorm LLC. . Retrieved 2009-09-08. "An improved Gigabaud Link Module (GLM) is provided for performing bi-directional data transfers between a host device and a serial transfer medium."
[6] http://www.microsoft.com/whdc
[7] http://www.linux-drivers.org
[8] http://www.rcnp.osaka-u.ac.jp/unix/DOCUMENTATION/HTML/AA-PUBVD-TE_html/TITLE.html
[9] http://linuxdriverproject.org/twiki/bin/view/Main/CompanyProcess
[10] http://www.kroah.com/log/linux/free_drivers_faq.html
[11] http://www.linuxhardware.org/
[12] http://lwn.net/Kernel/LDD3/

Advanced Configuration and Power Interface

In computing, the **Advanced Configuration and Power Interface** (**ACPI**) specification provides an open standard for unified operating system-centric device configuration and power management. ACPI, first released in December 1996, defines platform-independent interfaces for hardware discovery, configuration, power management and monitoring. The specification is central to *Operating System-directed configuration and Power Management* (OSPM); a term used to describe a system implementing ACPI, which therefore removes device management responsibilities from legacy firmware interfaces. The standard was originally developed by Intel, Microsoft, and Toshiba, and last published as "Revision 4.0a", on April 5, 2010. As of 2010, developers of ACPI also include HP and Phoenix.[1]

Overview

ACPI aims to consolidate and improve upon existing power and configuration standards for hardware devices.[1] It provides a transition from existing standards to entirely ACPI-compliant hardware, with some ACPI operating systems already removing support for legacy hardware.[2] With the intention of replacing Advanced Power Management, the MultiProcessor Specification and the Plug and Play BIOS Specification,[3] the standard brings power management into operating system control (OSPM), as opposed to the previous BIOS central system, which relied on platform-specific firmware to determine power management and configuration policy.[4]

The ACPI specification contains numerous related components for hardware and software programming, as well as a unified standard for device/power interaction and bus configuration. As a document that unifies many previous standards it covers many areas, for system and device builders as well as system programmers. Some software developers have trouble implementing ACPI and express concerns about the requirements that bytecode from an external source must be run by the system with full privileges.[5] Linus Torvalds, creator of the Linux kernel, once described it as "a complete design disaster in every way", in relation to his view that "modern PCs are horrible".[6]

Microsoft Windows 98 was the first operating system with full support for ACPI, with Windows 2000, Windows XP, Windows Vista, Windows 7, eComStation, FreeBSD, NetBSD, OpenBSD, HP-UX, OpenVMS, Linux and PC versions of SunOS all having at least some support for ACPI.

OSPM responsibilities

ACPI requires that once an OSPM-compatible operating system has activated ACPI on a computer, it then takes over and has exclusive control of all aspects of power management and device configuration. The OSPM implementation must expose an ACPI-compatible environment to device drivers, which exposes certain system, device and processor states.

Power States

Global states

The ACPI specification defines the following seven states (so-called global states) for an ACPI-compliant computer-system:

- **G0** (**S0**): *Working*
- **G1**, *Sleeping* subdivides into the four states S1 through S4:
  - **S1**: All processor caches are flushed, and the CPU(s) stop executing instructions. Power to the CPU(s) and RAM is maintained; devices that do not indicate they must remain on may be powered down.
  - **S2**: CPU powered off
  - **S3**: Commonly referred to as *Standby*, *Sleep*, or *Suspend to RAM*. RAM remains powered
  - **S4**: *Hibernation* or *Suspend to Disk*. All content of main memory is saved to non-volatile memory such as a hard drive, and is powered down.
- **G2** (**S5**), *Soft Off*: G2 is almost the same as G3 *Mechanical Off*, but some components remain powered so the computer can "wake" from input from the keyboard, clock, modem, LAN, or USB device.
- **G3**, *Mechanical Off*: The computer's power consumption approaches close to zero, to the point that the power cord can be removed and the system is safe for dis-assembly (typically, only the real-time clock is running off its own small battery).

Furthermore, the specification defines a *Legacy* state: the state on an operating system which does not support ACPI. In this state, the hardware and power are not managed via ACPI, effectively disabling ACPI.

Device states

The device states *D0-D3* are device-dependent:

- D0 *Fully-On* is the operating state.
- D1 and D2 are intermediate power-states whose definition varies by device.
- D3 *Off* has the device powered off and unresponsive to its bus.

Processor states

The CPU power states *C0-C3* are defined as follows:

- C0 is the operating state.
- C1 (often known as *Halt*) is a state where the processor is not executing instructions, but can return to an executing state essentially instantaneously. All ACPI-conformant processors must support this power state. Some processors, such as the Pentium 4, also support an Enhanced C1 state (C1E or Enhanced Halt State) for lower power consumption,[7] .
- C2 (often known as *Stop-Clock*) is a state where the processor maintains all software-visible state, but may take longer to wake up. This processor state is optional.
- C3 (often known as *Sleep*) is a state where the processor does not need to keep its cache coherent, but maintains other state. Some processors have variations on the C3 state (Deep Sleep, Deeper Sleep, etc.) that differ in how long it takes to wake the processor. This processor state is optional.

Performance states

While a device or processor operates (D0 and C0, respectively), it can be in one of several power-performance states. These states are implementation-dependent, but P0 is always the highest-performance state, with P1 to P*n* being successively lower-performance states, up to an implementation-specific limit of *n* no greater than 16.

P-states have become known as SpeedStep in Intel processors, as PowerNow! or Cool'n'Quiet in AMD processors, and as PowerSaver in VIA processors.

- P0 max power and frequency
- P1 less than P0, voltage/frequency scaled
- Pn less than P(n-1), voltage/frequency scaled

Hardware Interface

ACPI-compliant systems interact with hardware through either a "Function Fixed Hardware (FFH) Interface" or a platform-independent hardware programming model which relies on platform-specific AML provided by the Original Equipment Manufacturer.

Function Fixed Hardware Interfaces are platform-specific features, provided by platform manufacturers for the purposes of performance and failure recovery. Standard Intel-based PCs have a fixed function interface defined by Intel[8] , which provides a set of core functionality that reduces an ACPI-compliant system's need for full driver stacks for providing basic functionality during boot time or in the case of major system failure.

Firmware Interface

ACPI defines a large number of tables that provide the interface between an ACPI-compliant operating system and system firmware. These allow description of system hardware in a platform-independent manner, and are presented as either fixed formatted data structures or in ACPI Machine Language (AML). The main AML table is the DSDT (differentiated system description table).

The Root System Description Pointer is located in a platform-dependent manner, and describes the rest of the tables.

ACPI Component Architecture (ACPICA)

The ACPI Component Architecture (ACPICA) provides an open-source OS-independent reference implementation of the ACPI specification.[9]

Revision History

The first revision of the ACPI Specification was released in December 1996 supporting 16 and 32-bit addressing spaces. It wasn't until August 2000 that ACPI received 64-bit address support as well as support for multiprocessor workstations and servers with revision 2.0. In September 2004, revision 3.0 gave the ACPI specification support for SATA connectors, PCI Express bus, >256 multiprocessor support, ambient light sensors and user presence devices, as well as extending the Thermal model beyond the previous processor centric support. The latest of the major publications is that of revision 4.0. Released in June 2009, the 4.0 specification added many new features to the design; most notable are USB 3.0 support, logical processor idling support, and x2APIC support.[1]

See also

- Active State Power Management - hardware power management protocol for PCI Express
- Advanced Power Management (APM)
- Green computing
- Power management keys - Keyboard related
- Wake-on-LAN
- Wake-on-Ring
- Simple Firmware Interface (SFI)

External links

- Advanced Configuration and Power Interface Specification [10]
- ACPI home page [11]
- Intel's ACPI page [12]
- Intel's ACPI Component Architecture [13]
- How Linux Suspend and Resume works in the ACPI age [14]
- Everything You Need to Know About the CPU C-States Power Saving Modes [15]

This article was originally based on material from the Free On-line Dictionary of Computing, which is licensed under the GFDL.

References

[1] Intel Corporation, Hewlett-Packard, Microsoft, Toshiba, Phoenix Technologies (2010-05-05). "Advanced Configuration and Power Interface Specification, revision 4.0a" (http://www.acpi.info/DOWNLOADS/ACPIspec40a.pdf) (PDF). . Retrieved 2010-07-02.

[2] Marshall, Allen. "ACPI in Windows Vista" (http://download.microsoft.com/download/5/b/9/5b97017b-e28a-4bae-ba48-174cf47d23cd/CPA002_WH06.ppt) (PPT). Microsoft Corporation. . Retrieved 2010-07-02.

[3] ACPI Overview (http://www.acpi.info/presentations/ACPI_Overview.pdf)

[4] Microsoft Corporation, Intel Corporation (February 1996). "APM BIOS Specification" (http://download.microsoft.com/download/1/6/1/161ba512-40e2-4cc9-843a-923143f3456c/APMV12.rtf). Microsoft Corporation. . Retrieved 2010-07-02.

[5] Corbet, Jonathan (2001-07-04). "Kernel development" (http://lwn.net/2001/0704/kernel.php3). *LWN.net weekly edition*. LWN.net. . Retrieved 2010-07-02.

[6] Searls, Doc (2003-11-25). "Linus & the Lunatics, Part II" (http://www.linuxjournal.com/article/7279). Linux Journal. . Retrieved 2010-01-13.

[7] Wasson, Scott (2005-02-21). "Intel's Pentium 4 600 series processors" (http://techreport.com/articles.x/7998/2). The Tech Report. p. 2. .

[8] Intel Corporation (September 2006). "Intel Processor Vendor-Specific ACPI" (ftp://download.intel.com/technology/iapc/acpi/downloads/30222305.pdf) (PDF). . Retrieved 2010-07-02.

[9] ACPICA (http://www.acpica.org/)

[10] http://www.acpi.info/DOWNLOADS/ACPIspec40.pdf?bcsi_scan_2732326C0C392ABB=0&bcsi_scan_filename=ACPIspec40.pdf

[11] http://www.acpi.info/

[12] http://www.intel.com/technology/iapc/acpi/

[13] http://www.acpica.org/

[14] http://www.advogato.org/article/913.html

[15] http://www.hardwaresecrets.com/article/611

Device driver

In computing, a **device driver** or **software driver** is a computer program allowing higher-level computer programs to interact with a hardware device.

A driver typically communicates with the device through the computer bus or communications subsystem to which the hardware connects. When a calling program invokes a routine in the driver, the driver issues commands to the device. Once the device sends data back to the driver, the driver may invoke routines in the original calling program. Drivers are hardware-dependent and operating-system-specific. They usually provide the interrupt handling required for any necessary asynchronous time-dependent hardware interface.

Purpose

A device driver simplifies programming by acting as a translator between a hardware device and the applications or operating systems that use it. Programmers can write the higher-level application code independently of whatever specific hardware device it will ultimately control, because code and device can interface in a standard way, regardless of the software superstructure or of underlying hardware. Every version of a device, such as a printer, requires its own hardware-specific specialized commands. In contrast, most applications utilize devices (such as a file to a printer) by means of high-level device-generic commands such as PRINTLN (print a line). The device-driver accepts these generic high-level commands and breaks them into a series of low-level device-specific commands as required by the device being driven. Furthermore, drivers can provide a level of security as they can run in kernel-mode, thereby protecting the operating system from applications running in user-mode.

Design

Device drivers can be abstracted into logical and physical layers. Logical layers process data for a class of devices such as Ethernet ports or disk drives. Physical layers communicate with specific device instances. For example, a serial port needs to handle standard communication protocols such as XON/XOFF that are common for all serial port hardware. This would be managed by a serial port logical layer. However, the physical layer needs to communicate with a particular serial port chip. 16550 UART hardware differs from PL-011. The physical layer addresses these chip-specific variations. Conventionally, OS requests go to the logical layer first. In turn, the logical layer calls upon the physical layer to implement OS requests in terms understandable by the hardware. Inversely, when a hardware device needs to respond to the OS, it uses the physical layer to speak to the logical layer.

In Linux environments, programmers can build device drivers either as parts of the kernel or separately as loadable modules. Makedev includes a list of the devices in Linux: ttyS (terminal), lp (parallel port), hd (disk), loop (loopback disk device), sound (these include mixer, sequencer, dsp, and audio)... [1]

The Microsoft Windows .sys files and Linux .ko modules contain loadable device drivers. The advantage of loadable device drivers is that they can be loaded only when necessary and then unloaded, thus saving kernel memory.

Development

Writing a device driver requires an in-depth understanding of how the hardware and the software of a given platform function. Drivers operate in a highly privileged environment and can cause disaster if they get things wrong.[2] In contrast, most user-level software on modern operating systems can be stopped without greatly affecting the rest of the system. Even drivers executing in user mode can crash a system if the device is erroneously programmed. These factors make it more difficult and dangerous to diagnose problems.

Thus the task of writing drivers usually falls to software engineers who work for hardware-development companies. This is because they have better information than most outsiders about the design of their hardware. Moreover, it was traditionally considered in the hardware manufacturer's interest to guarantee that their clients can use their hardware in an optimum way. Typically, the *logical device driver* (LDD) is written by the operating system vendor, while the *physical device driver* (PDD) is implemented by the device vendor. But in recent years non-vendors have written numerous device drivers, mainly for use with free and open source operating systems. In such cases, it is important that the hardware manufacturer provides information on how the device communicates. Although this information can instead be learned by reverse engineering, this is much more difficult with hardware than it is with software.

Microsoft has attempted to reduce system instability due to poorly written device drivers by creating a new framework for driver development, called Windows Driver Foundation (WDF). This includes User-Mode Driver Framework (UMDF) that encourages development of certain types of drivers — primarily those that implement a message-based protocol for communicating with their devices — as user mode drivers. If such drivers malfunction, they do not cause system instability. The Kernel-Mode Driver Framework (KMDF) model continues to allow development of kernel-mode device drivers, but attempts to provide standard implementations of functions that are well known to cause problems, including cancellation of I/O operations, power management, and plug and play device support.

Apple has an open-source framework for developing drivers on Mac OS X called the I/O Kit.

Kernel-mode vs user-mode

Device drivers, particularly on modern Windows platforms, can run in kernel-mode (Ring 0) or in user-mode (Ring 3).[3] The primary benefit of running a driver in user mode is improved stability, since a poorly written user mode device driver cannot crash the system by overwriting kernel memory.[4] On the other hand, user/kernel-mode transitions usually impose a considerable performance overhead, thereby prohibiting user mode-drivers for low latency and high throughput requirements.

Kernel space can be accessed by user module only through the use of system calls. End user programs like the UNIX shell or other GUI based applications are part of the user space. These applications interact with hardware through kernel supported functions.

Applications

Because of the diversity of modern hardware and operating systems, drivers operate in many different environments. Drivers may interface with:

- printers
- video adapters
- network cards
- Sound cards
- local buses of various sorts — in particular, for bus mastering on modern systems
- low-bandwidth I/O buses of various sorts (for pointing devices such as mice, keyboards, USB, etc.)
- computer storage devices such as hard disk, CD-ROM and floppy disk buses (ATA, SATA, SCSI)
- implementing support for different file systems
- image scanners
- digital cameras

Common levels of abstraction for device drivers include:

- for hardware:
  - interfacing directly
  - writing to or reading from a device control register
  - using some higher-level interface (e.g. Video BIOS)

- using another lower-level device driver (e.g. file system drivers using disk drivers)
- simulating work with hardware, while doing something entirely different
- for software:
  - allowing the operating system direct access to hardware resources
  - implementing only primitives
  - implementing an interface for non-driver software (e.g. TWAIN)
  - implementing a language, sometimes quite high-level (e.g. PostScript)

Choosing and installing the correct device drivers for given hardware is often a key component of computer system configuration.

Virtual device drivers

Virtual device drivers represent a particular variant of device drivers. They are used to emulate a hardware device, particularly in virtualization environments, for example when a DOS program is run on a Microsoft Windows computer or when a guest operating system is run on, for example, a Xen host. Instead of enabling the guest operating system to dialog with hardware, virtual device drivers take the opposite role and emulate a piece of hardware, so that the guest operating system and its drivers running inside a virtual machine can have the illusion of accessing real hardware. Attempts by the guest operating system to access the hardware are routed to the virtual device driver in the host operating system as e.g. function calls. The virtual device driver can also send simulated processor-level events like interrupts into the virtual machine.

Virtual devices may also operate in a non-virtualized environment. For example a virtual network adapter is used with a virtual private network, while a virtual disk device is used with iSCSI.

Open drivers

- Printers: CUPS
- Scanners: SANE
- Video: Vidix, Direct Rendering Infrastructure

Solaris descriptions of commonly-used device drivers

- fas: Fast/wide SCSI controller
- hme: Fast (10/100 Mbit/s) Ethernet
- isp: Differential SCSI controllers and the SunSwift card
- glm: (Gigabaud Link Module[5]) UltraSCSI controllers
- scsi: Small Computer Serial Interface (SCSI) devices
- sf: soc+ or socal Fiber Channel Arbitrated Loop (FCAL)
- soc: SPARC Storage Array (SSA) controllers
- socal: Serial optical controllers for FCAL (soc+)

APIs

- Advanced Linux Sound Architecture (ALSA) - as of 2009 the standard Linux sound-driver interface
- I/O Kit - an open-source framework from Apple for developing Mac OS X device drivers
- Installable File System (IFS) - a filesystem API for IBM OS/2 and Microsoft Windows NT
- Network Driver Interface Specification (NDIS) - a standard network card driver API
- Open Data-Link Interface (ODI) - a network card API similar to NDIS
- Scanner Access Now Easy (SANE) - a public-domain interface to raster-image scanner-hardware
- Uniform Driver Interface (UDI) - a cross-platform driver interface project
- Windows Display Driver Model (WDDM) - the graphic display driver architecture for Windows Vista
- Windows Driver Foundation (WDF)
- Windows Driver Model (WDM)

Identifiers

- Device id is the device identifier and Vendor id is the vendor identifier.

See also

- Class driver
- Firmware
- Interrupt
- Loadable kernel module
- Makedev
- Open-source hardware
- Printer driver
- udev

External links

- Microsoft Windows Hardware Developer Central [6]
- Linux Hardware Compatibility Lists and Linux Drivers [7]
- Writing Device Drivers: A Tutorial [8]
- If you wish to have Linux drivers written for your device [9]
- Free Linux Driver Development Questions and Answers [10]
- Linux hardware [11]
- O'Reilly e-book: Linux Device Drivers, Third Edition [12]

zs:驱动程序

References

[1] "MAKEDEV — Linux Command — Unix Command" (http://linux.about.com/od/commands/l/blcmdl8_MAKEDEV.htm). Linux.about.com. 2009-09-11. . Retrieved 2009-09-17.

[2] "Device Driver Basics" (http://www.linux-tutorial.info/modules.php?name=Tutorial&pageid=255). .

[3] "User-mode vs. Kernel-mode Drivers" (http://technet2.microsoft.com/windowsserver/en/library/eb1936c0-e19c-4a17-a1a8-39292e4929a41033.mspx?mfr=true). Microsoft. 2003-03-01. . Retrieved 2008-03-04.

[4] "Introduction to the User-Mode Driver Framework (UMDF)" (http://blogs.msdn.com/iliast/archive/2006/10/10/Introduction-to-the-User_2D00_Mode-Driver-Framework.aspx). Microsoft. 2006-10-10. . Retrieved 2008-03-04.

[5] "US Patent 5969841 - Gigabaud link module with received power detect signal" (http://www.patentstorm.us/patents/5969841.html). PatentStorm LLC. . Retrieved 2009-09-08. "An improved Gigabaud Link Module (GLM) is provided for performing bi-directional data transfers between a host device and a serial transfer medium."

ATI Catalyst

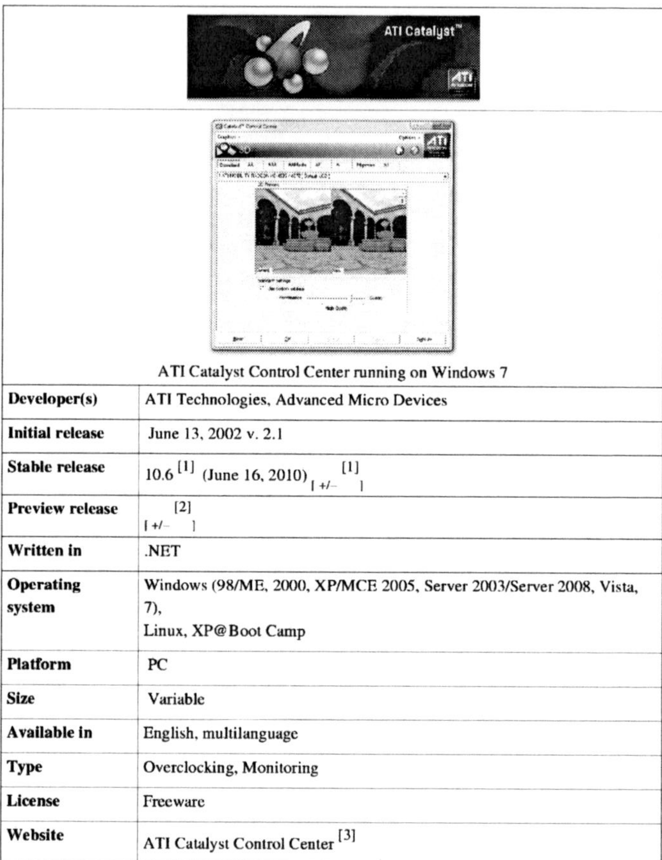

ATI Catalyst Control Center running on Windows 7

Developer(s)	ATI Technologies, Advanced Micro Devices
Initial release	June 13, 2002 v. 2.1
Stable release	10.6 [1] (June 16, 2010) [1] [+/−]
Preview release	[2] [+/−]
Written in	.NET
Operating system	Windows (98/ME, 2000, XP/MCE 2005, Server 2003/Server 2008, Vista, 7), Linux, XP@Boot Camp
Platform	PC
Size	Variable
Available in	English, multilanguage
Type	Overclocking, Monitoring
License	Freeware
Website	ATI Catalyst Control Center [3]

ATI Catalyst is a utility software driver package for ATI Radeon products for Microsoft Windows operating systems and Linux, on 32- and 64-bit x86 processors. The Catalyst software was instituted on 13 June 2002 [4] with version 02.1 after the release of the Radeon 8500, as "a software suite that includes unified driver and software applications to enable [ATI's] Radeon family of graphics products" for Windows XP, Windows 2000 and Windows Me, with support for Windows 98 via the Windows Me driver. The first number in a release version denotes the year, the second the release within that year, starting at x.1 for all years other than 2003 when there was a 3.0 release.

The original release of the Catalyst suite consisted of four software elements: a new, unified driver for ATI's Radeon graphics cards; Hydravision, ATI's proprietary desktop management software; an ATI "Multimedia Center", and ATI's Remote Wonder software, as well as a new AGP diagnostic and stability tool, and a newly redesigned control panel. Key features promised by ATI include frequent (now monthly) driver updates with performance enhancements, bug fixes, and new features.

Support for DOS-based versions of Windows was dropped with the 4.4 release on 7 April 2004, although there were some later non-WHQL releases for these operating systems, including and up to a Windows Me build of Catalyst 6.2

released on 9 February 2006. Support for Windows 2000 was dropped from releases after 6.5[5] . Support for Windows Vista was added in 7.2[6] on 22 February 2007, and support for Windows XP x64 edition was added on 21 November 2007 in 7.11[7] . Support for Windows 7 was added in 9.7[8] on 23 July 2009.

From the 4.9 release on 4 September 2004, the Catalyst driver package included by default the ATI Catalyst Control Center [9] , a new interface for manipulating many of the hardware's functions, such as 3D settings, monitor controls, and video options, and offering a small 3D preview allowing the user to see how changes to the graphics settings affected the quality of the rendered image. This software requires Microsoft's .NET Framework to be installed, and allows for adjustments to the Radeon card as well as for showing information about the card itself and the software data. There are three modes for the control center: simple, advanced and wizard modes. A version of the driver is available without this control center.

From the release of Catalyst 7.11[10] , the ATI Proprietry Linux driver was renamed ATI Catalyst Linux, and moved to the same release dates and version numbering as the versions for Microsoft Windows.

Graphic settings

- Monitor properties
  - Multiple monitor – Additional monitor running in either extended desktop mode or desktop replication
  - HDTV support – Setting display resolutions (720p/1080i/1080p) and refresh rates (60 Hz to 85 Hz) to fit HDTV connected via component or HDMI
- 3D settings – such as Anti-aliasing and Anisotropic filtering
- ATI Avivo – hardware acceleration of video decoding includes a set of video settings like gamma correction, only applies to the Radeon X1000 series, HD 2000/3000 series, and HD 4000 series
- SmartGart (available to AGP products only)
- VPU Recovery – Resets graphics processor in case it no longer responds to display driver
- ATI Overdrive – Overclocking of video cards to enhance performance
- ATI PowerPlay – Adjust power saving plans to the GPU, only applies to Mobility Radeon, Radeon HD 3800 series and Radeon HD4800 Series
- ATI CrossFireX – Manages the use of multiple graphics cards bridged with ATI's proprietary CrossFireX standard.

Supported products

- ATI Radeon graphics cards
  - Monthly updated:
    - Radeon HD 2000/3000 series
    - Radeon HD 4000 series
    - Radeon HD 5000 series
  - Aperiodicity updated: - With no Official Windows 7 Support
    - Radeon 9500/9550/9600/9700/9800/X300/X500/X600 series
    - Radeon X1500/X1600/X1800/X1900 series
- ATI multimedia products
  - All-in-Wonder multimedia cards
    - All-in-Wonder HD
    - All-in-Wonder 2006 Edition
    - All-in-Wonder X1800/X1900 series
    - All-in-Wonder X800 series
    - All-in-Wonder X600 series

        - All-in-Wonder 9600/9800 series
    - Theater HDTV decoders
        - Theater 600
        - Theater HD 750
        - Theater 550 PRO
        - Theater 650
- AMD FireStream products
    - FireStream 9270
    - FireStream 9170
    - FireStream 9250
- AMD integrated graphics processors
    - Radeon HD 4200/3000 series
    - 690 chipset series/Radeon X1200 series/Radeon Xpress 1200 series
    - 580X chipset series
    - Radeon Xpress 3200 CrossFire
    - Radeon Xpress 200/1100/1150 series

See also

- Radeon
- Comparison of ATI chipsets
- Comparison of AMD chipsets
- All-in-Wonder
- Graphics hardware and FOSS

External links

- ATI Catalyst Control Center [3]
- ATI Driver support [11]
- AMD Game Driver Page [12]

References

[1] http://en.wikipedia.org/wiki/Template%3Alatest_stable_software_release%2Fati_catalyst
[2] http://en.wikipedia.org/wiki/Template%3Alatest_preview_software_release%2Fati_catalyst
[3] http://ati.amd.com/products/catalystcontrolcenter/index.html
[4] ATI Catalyst announcement (http://ati.amd.com/companyinfo/press/2002/4506.html)
[5] ATI Catalyst 6.6 release notes (http://www2.ati.com/relnotes/catalyst_66_release_notes.html)
[6] ATI Catalyst 7.2 release notes (http://www2.ati.com/relnotes/catalyst_72_release_notes.html)
[7] ATI Catalyst 7.11 release notes (http://www2.ati.com/relnotes/catalyst_711_release_notes.html)
[8] ATI Catalyst 9.7 release notes (http://www2.ati.com/relnotess/Catalyst_97_release_notes.pdf)
[9] ATI Catalyst Control Center announcement (http://ati.amd.com/companyinfo/press/2004/4776.html)
[10] ATI Catalyst Linux 7.11 release notes (http://www2.ati.com/drivers/linux/catalyst_711_linux.html)
[11] http://ati.amd.com/support/driver.html
[12] http://game.amd.com/us-en/drivers_catalyst.aspx

Advanced SCSI Programming Interface

ASPI, the **Advanced SCSI Programming Interface** provides an API originated by Adaptec which standardizes communication on a computer bus between a SCSI host adapter on the one hand and SCSI (and ATAPI) peripherals on the other.

History

ASPI was developed by Adaptec in the early 1990s. It was originally designed to support SCSI drives. Support for ATAPI interface (such as IDE) was later added.

Microsoft licensed the interface for use with Windows 9x series. At the same time Microsoft developed SCSI Pass Through Interface (SPTI), an in-house substitute that worked on the NT platform. Microsoft did not include ASPI in Windows 2000/XP, in favor of its own SPTI. Users may still download ASPI from Adaptec. A number of CD/DVD applications also continue to offer their own implementations of ASPI layer.

Driver

ASPI was provided by the following drivers.

Operating System	Driver Filename	Bundled
DOS	ASPI4DOS.SYS	No
Windows 3.1x	WINASPI.DLL	No
Windows 95, 98 and ME	WNASPI32.DLL, WINASPI.DLL, APIX.VXD and ASPIENUM.VXD	Yes
Windows NT, 2000, XP	WNASPI32.DLL, ASPI32.SYS	No
FreeDOS	USBASPI.SYS	Unknown

See also

- SCSI Pass-Through Direct (SPTD)
- SCSI Pass Through Interface (SPTI)

External links

Adaptec's ASPI driver

- Windows ASPI Package [1]

Non-Adaptec implementations

- Pinnacle Systems's ASAPI driver [2]
- Nero's ASPI driver [3]
- Frog Aspi [4]
- MekugiAspi [5]

Technical information

- Technical reference (ASPI for Win32) [6]
- ASPI Layer setup [7]

References

[1] http://www.adaptec.com/en-US/speed/software_pc/aspi/aspi_471a2_exe.htm
[2] ftp://ftp.pinnaclesys.de/driver/pc/InstantCDDVD/ASAPI.exe
[3] ftp://ftp6.nero.com/NeroASPIdt.exe
[4] http://www.frogaspi.org/download.htm
[5] http://come.to/t_chan/MekugiAspi/MekugiAspi.htm
[6] http://www.zianet.com/jgray/dat/files/ASPI32.pdf
[7] http://www.doom9.org/aspi.htm

Airjack (device driver)

AirJack is a device driver (or suite of device drivers) for IEEE 802.11(a/b/g) raw frame injection and reception. It is meant as a development tool for all manner of 802.11 applications that need to access the raw protocol.

External links

- http://www.sourceforge.net

BNU (software)

BNU is a high-performance communications device driver designed to provide enhanced support for serial port communications. The BNU serial port driver was specifically targeted for use with early (late 1980s - 1990's) DOS-based BBS software. The reason for BNU and other similar enhanced serial port drivers was to provide better support for serial communications software than what was offered by the machine's BIOS and/or DOS being used on the machine. Having serial port support as provided by BNU and other similar drivers allowed the communications software programmers to spend more time on the actual applications instead of the depths and details of how to talk to the serial ports and the modems connected to them. Sending communications data across a modem link was a lot more involved than sending data to a serial printer which was basically all that was originally capable of being done with the existing serial port software support.

BNU was written by David Nugent as an experimental driver for serial communications following the FOSSIL specification. David released BNU to the public in 1989 and its use in the BBS world spread rapidly. BNU was one of only two or three available FOSSIL drivers for the IBM PC compatible hardware and MS/PC-DOS operating system. Because of this, BNU has been one of the most widely used MS-DOS FOSSIL communications drivers.

BNU was mainly used with DOS-based Bulletin Board System (BBS) software written in the late 1980s to mid 1990's. It is not used by Windows-based BBS software, but BNU can be used under Windows NTVDM to run DOS-based BBS software under Windows. BNU and other similar drivers were not limited solely to being used in the BBS world. The enhanced capabilities they offered were also used to easily communicate with other serially connected devices for the same reasons that the FOSSIL specification and FOSSIL drivers were originally created. That reason, as noted above, was to separate the details of serial port communications from the actual application. The software's programmers only needed to talk to the serial driver in a standardized way to send and receive their data.

The name "BNU" was originally a rip-off of AT&T's "BNU UUCP", and in that context meant "Basic Networking Utilities". The author of BNU, David Nugent, felt that the acronym was particularly apt for BNU's function. BNU was also called "Bloody Nugent's Utility" because it was written by David Nugent as one of his many BBS related utilities and it was not known at the time what the acronym "BNU" actually stood for.

The BNUFAQ [1] used to be posted in the Fidonet BNU support echo by the author. This saved text file is the last official posting of this FAQ by David Nugent, BNU's author.

References

[1] http://www.wpusa.dynip.com/files2/FOSSIL/BNUFAQ.TXT

Broadcast Driver Architecture

The **Broadcast Driver Architecture** (BDA) is a Microsoft standard for digital video capture on Microsoft Windows operating systems. It encompasses the ATSC and DVB standards and gives developers a standardized method of accessing TV tuner devices (usually PCI, PCI-E or USB). It is the driver component of Microsoft TV Technologies, and is used by hardware vendors to create digital TV tuning devices for Windows, and also to support new network types or custom hardware functionality. BDA is documented in the Windows DDK (Driver Development Kit) and the Platform SDK. Ideally, any BDA-compliant software should be compatible with any BDA-compliant hardware.

Applications using BDA drivers include Web TV for Windows (built into Windows 98 and Windows Me), Windows XP Media Center Edition, MediaPortal, GB-PVR, DVBViewer, ULENet [1] and several such other third-party solutions.

Broadcast Driver Architecture was introduced in Windows 98 as part of the Windows Driver Model.

See also

- Windows Driver Model

External links

- Microsoft TV and Broadcast Driver Architecture [2]
- Protected Broadcast Driver Architecture [3] Extensions to BDA for DRM
- Microsoft BDA Reference [4]
- Open Source BDA drivers and tools [5]

References

[1] http://network-research.org/ulenet/ulenet.html
[2] http://www.microsoft.com/whdc/archive/broadcast.mspx
[3] http://www.microsoft.com/whdc/device/stream/BDA_protect.mspx
[4] http://msdn2.microsoft.com/en-us/library/ms779699.aspx
[5] http://sourceforge.net/projects/bdadev/

CEN/XFS

CEN/XFS or **XFS** provides a client-server architecture for financial applications on the Microsoft Windows platform, especially peripheral devices such as EFTPOS terminals and ATMs which are unique to the financial industry. It was initially known as **WOSA Extensions for Financial Services** or **WOSA/XFS**.

With the move to a more standardized software base, financial institutions have been increasingly interested in the ability to pick and choose the application programs that drive their equipment. XFS provides a common API for accessing and manipulating various financial services devices regardless of the manufacturer.

History

Chronology:

- 1991 - Microsoft forms "Banking Solutions Vendor Council"
- 1995 - WOSA/XFS 1.11 released
- 1997 - WOSA/XFS 2.0 released - additional support for 24 hours-a-day unattended operation
- 1998 - adopted by CEN as an international standard.
- 2000 - XFS 3.0 released by CEN
- 2008 - XFS 3.10 released by CEN

WOSA/XFS changed name to simply XFS when the standard was adopted by the international CEN/ISSS standards body. However, it is most commonly called CEN/XFS by the industry participants.

XFS Middleware

While the perceived benefit of XFS is similar to Java's "Write once, run anywhere" mantra, often different hardware vendors have different interpretations of the XFS standard. The result of these differences in interpretation means that applications typically use a middleware to even out the differences between various platforms implementation of XFS.

Notable XFS middleware platforms include:

- Hitachi-Omron Terminal Solutions ATOM
- Diebold Agilis Power
- NCR Corporation Aptra Edge
- KAL Kalignite
- Phoenix Interactive VISTAatm
- Wincor Nixdorf Protopas
- SBS Software KIXFS/Terminal Control
- Dynasty Technology Group - (JSI) Jam Service Interface
- HST Systems & Technologies - HAL Interface
- FreeXFS [1]- Open source XFS platform

XFS Test Tools

XFS test tools allow testing of XFS applications and middleware on simulated hardware. Some tools include sophisticated automatic regression testing capabilities.

Providers of XFS test tools include:

- Level Four Software Ltd, BRIDGE:test
- KAL Kalignite Test Utilities
- Lexcel TestSystem ATM - Open Architecture
- Dynasty Technology Group - JSI Simulators
- HST Systems & Technologies (Brazil)
- Software Industries Ltd, XFS Explorer [2]

Related links

- J/XFS - a Java alternative to the CEN/XFS standard.[3]
- Xpeak - Devices Connectivity using XML (Open Source Project).
- Automated teller machine
- Teller assist unit
- List of companies involved with ATMs

External links

- CEN/XFS Home Page [4]
- CEN/XFS ATM Software Info [5]
- WOSA/XFS driver developers (http://www.nayadegroup.com) Spanish [6]
- Dynasty Technology Group S.A. [7]

References

[1] http://code.google.com/p/freexfs/
[2] http://software-industries.com/products-xfs_explorer.htm
[3] J/XFS Web Site - Welcome to J/XFS (http://jxfs.net/)
[4] http://www.cen.eu/cenorm/sectors/sectors/isss/activity/bankingsoftware.asp
[5] http://www.cen-xfs-atm-software.info
[6] http://www.nayadegroup.com
[7] http://www.dynasty.es

Class driver

In computing, a **class driver** is a type of hardware device driver that can operate a large number of different devices of a broadly similar type.

Class drivers are very often used with USB based devices, which share the essential USB protocol in common, and devices with similar functionality can easily adopt common protocols.

As another example, instead of having a separate driver for every kind of CD-ROM device, a class driver can operate a wide variety of CD-ROMs from different manufacturers. To accomplish this the manufacturers make their products compatible with a standardized protocol.

In technical terms, a class driver is used as a base or ancestor class for specific drivers which need to have slightly different or extended functionality, but which can take advantage of the majority of the functionality provided by the class driver. This concept is a key aspect of object oriented programming, which when extended to drivers makes it much easier for hardware vendors to provide driver support for their products.

See also

- Windows Driver Model
- USB video device class
- USB device classes

External links

- Microsoft USB class driver discussion [1]
- Jungo - Host Class Drivers [2]
- Mac OS X class driver information from Apple [3]
- Linux gadget drivers [4]

References

[1] http://www.microsoft.com/whdc/device/input/smartcard/USB_CCID.mspx#E5
[2] http://www.jungo.com/st/drivercore_pc_usb_communication_drivers.html
[3] http://developer.apple.com/qa/qa2004/qa1370.html
[4] http://www.linux-usb.org/gadget/

CUPS

Original author(s)	Michael Sweet (Easy Software Products)
Developer(s)	Apple Inc.
Initial release	June 9, 1999
Stable release	1.4.4 / June 17, 2010
Operating system	Unix-like
Type	Print server
License	GNU General Public License, GNU Lesser General Public License, with proprietary exceptions for software that links against CUPS to run on Apple operating systems [1]
Website	http://www.cups.org

CUPS (formerly an acronym for Common Unix Printing System), a modular printing system for Unix-like computer operating systems, allows a computer to act as a print server. A computer running CUPS is a host that can accept print jobs from client computers, process them, and send them to the appropriate printer.

CUPS consists of a print spooler and scheduler, a filter system that converts the print data to a format that the printer will understand, and a backend system that sends this data to the print device. CUPS uses the Internet Printing Protocol (IPP) as the basis for managing print jobs and queues. It also provides the traditional command line interfaces for the System V and Berkeley print systems, and provides support for the Berkeley print system's Line Printer Daemon protocol and limited support for the server message block (SMB) protocol. System administrators can configure the device drivers which CUPS supplies by editing text files in Adobe's PostScript Printer Description (PPD) format. There are a number of user interfaces for different platforms that can configure CUPS, and it has a built-in web-based interface. CUPS is free software, provided under the GNU General Public License and GNU Lesser General Public License, Version 2.

History

Michael Sweet, who owns Easy Software Products, started developing CUPS in 1997. The first public betas appeared in 1999.[2] The original design of CUPS used the LPD protocol, but due to limitations in LPD and vendor incompatibilities, the Internet Printing Protocol (IPP) was chosen instead. CUPS was quickly adopted as the default printing system for several Linux distributions, including Red Hat Linux. In March 2002, Apple Inc. adopted CUPS as the printing system for Mac OS X 10.2.[3] In February 2007, Apple Inc. hired chief developer Michael Sweet and purchased the CUPS source code.[4]

Overview

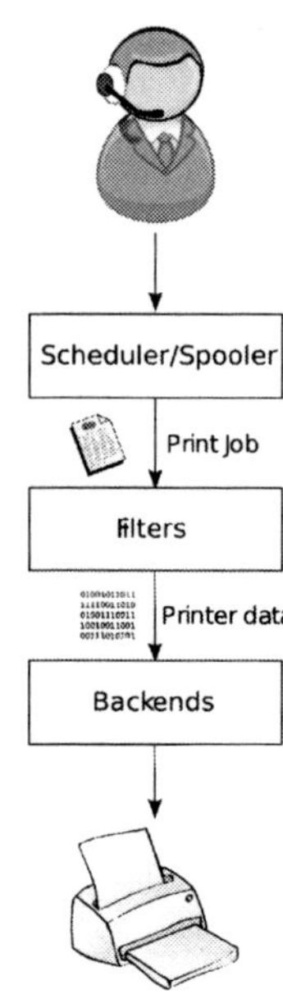

CUPS provides a mechanism that allows print jobs to be sent to printers in a standard fashion. The print-data goes to a *scheduler*[5] which sends jobs to a *filter system* that converts the print job into a format the printer will understand.[6] The filter system then passes the data on to a *backend*—a special filter that sends print data to a device or network connection.[7] The system makes extensive use of PostScript and rasterization of data to convert the data into a format suitable for the destination printer.

CUPS offers a standard and modularised printing system that can process numerous data formats on the print server. Before CUPS, it was difficult to find a standard printer management system that would accommodate the very wide variety of printers on the market using their own printer languages and formats. For instance, the System V and Berkeley printing systems were largely incompatible with each other, and they required complicated scripts and workarounds to convert the program's data format to a printable format. They often could not detect the file format that was being sent to the printer and thus could not automatically and correctly convert the data stream. Additionally, data conversion was performed on individual workstations rather than a central server.

CUPS allows printer manufacturers and printer-driver developers to more easily create drivers that work natively on the print server. Processing occurs on the server, allowing for easier network-based printing than with other Unix printing systems. With Samba installed, users can address printers on remote Windows computers and generic PostScript drivers can be used for printing across the network.

Scheduler

The CUPS scheduler implements Internet Printing Protocol (IPP) over HTTP/1.1. A helper application (cups-lpd) converts Line Printer Daemon protocol (LPD) requests to IPP. The scheduler also provides a web-based interface for managing print jobs, the configuration of the server, and for documentation about CUPS itself.[5]

An *authorization* module controls which IPP and HTTP messages can pass through the system.[8] Once the IPP/HTTP packets are authorised they are sent to the *client* module, which listens for and processes incoming connections. The client module is also responsible for executing external CGI programs as needed to support web-based printers, classes, and job status monitoring and administration.[9] Once this module has processed its requests, it sends them to the *IPP* module which performs Uniform Resource Identifier (URI) validation to prevent a client from sidestepping any access controls or authentication on the HTTP server.[10] The URI is a text string that indicates a name or address that can be used to refer to an abstract or physical resource on a network.

The scheduler allows for classes of printers. Applications can send requests to groups of printers in a class, allowing the scheduler to direct the job to the first available printer in that class.[11] A *jobs* module manages print jobs, sending them to the filter and backend processes for final conversion and printing, and monitoring the status messages from those processes.[12]

The CUPS scheduler utilizes a *configuration* module, which parses configuration files, initializes CUPS data structures, and starts and stops the CUPS program. The configuration module will stop CUPS services during configuration file processing and then restart the service when processing is complete.[13]

A *logging* module handles the logging of scheduler events for access, error, and page log files. The *main* module handles timeouts and dispatch of I/O requests for client connections, watching for signals, handling child process errors and exits, and reloading the server configuration files as needed.[14]

Other modules used by the scheduler include:

- the *MIME* module, which handles a Multipurpose Internet Mail Extensions (MIME) type and conversion database used in the filtering process that converts print data to a format suitable for a print device;[15]
- a *PPD* module that handles a list of Postscript Printer Description (PPD) files;[16]
- a *devices* module that manages a list of devices that are available in the system;[17]
- a *printers* module that handles printers and PPDs within CUPS.[18]

Filter system

CUPS can process a variety of data formats on the print server. It converts the print-job data into the final language/format of the printer via a series of *filters*.[19] [20] It uses MIME types for identifying file formats.

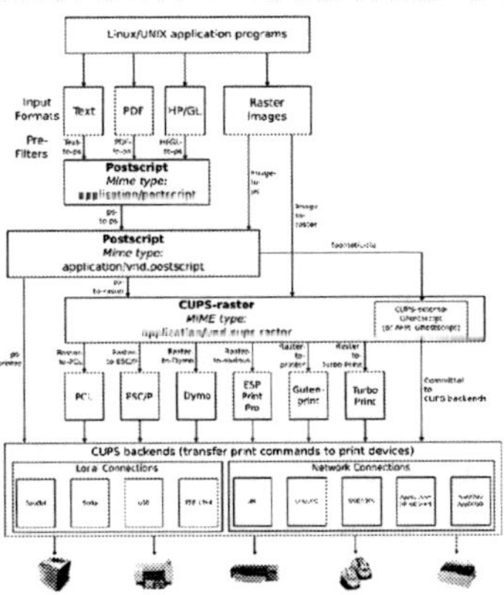

CUPS allows users to send different data to the CUPS server and have that data converted into a format the printer will understand and be able to print

MIME databases

After the CUPS system has assigned the print job to the scheduler, it is passed to the CUPS filter system. This converts the data to a format suitable for the printer. During start-up, the CUPS daemon loads two MIME databases: mime.types that defines the known file types that CUPS can accept data for, and mime.convs that defines the programs that process each particular MIME type.[21]

The mime.types file has the syntax:

mimetype { [file-extensions] | [pattern-match] }

For example, to detect an HTML file, the following entry would be applicable:

text/html html htm \

printable(0,1024) + (string(0,"<HTML>") string(0,"<!DOCTYPE"))

The second line matches the file contents to the specified MIME type by determining that the first kilobyte of text in the file holds printable characters and that those characters include html markup. If the pattern above matches, then the filter system would mark the file as the MIME type text/html.[22]

The mime.convs file has the syntax:

source destination cost program

The *source* field designates the MIME type that is determined by looking up the mime.types file, while the *destination* field lists the type of output requested and determines what program should be used. This is also retrieved from mime.types. The *cost* field assists in the selection of sets of filters when converting a file. The last field, *program*, determines which filter program to use to perform the data conversion.[23]

Some examples:

```
text/plain application/postscript 50 texttops
application/vnd.cups-postscript application/vnd.cups-raster 50 pstoraster
image/* application/vnd.cups-postscript 50 imagetops
image/* application/vnd.cups-raster 50 imagetoraster
```

Filtering process

The filtering process works by taking input data pre-formatted with six arguments:

1. the job ID of the print job
2. the user-name
3. the job-name
4. the number of copies to print
5. any print options
6. the filename (though this is unnecessary if it is has been redirected from standard input).[20]

It then determines the type of data that is being input and the filter to be used through the use of the MIME databases, for instance image data will be detected and processed through a particular filter and HTML data detected and processed through another filter.

CUPS can convert supplied data either into PostScript data or directly into raster data. If it is converted into PostScript data an additional filter is applied called a *prefilter*, which runs the PostScript data through another PostScript converter so that it can add printer specific options like selecting page ranges to print, setting *n*-up mode and other device-specific things.[24] After the pre-filtering is done, the data can either be sent directly to a CUPS backend if using a PostScript printer, or it can be passed to another filter like Foomatic by linuxprinting.org. Alternatively, it can be passed to Ghostscript, which converts the PostScript into an intermediary *CUPS-raster* format.[25] The intermediary raster format is then passed onto a final filter which converts the raster data to a printer-specific format. The default filters included with CUPS include:

- raster to PCL
- raster to ESC/P or ESC/P2 (an Epson printer language, now largely superseded by their new ESC/P-Raster format)
- raster to Dymo (another printer company).
- raster to Zebra Programming Language or ZPL (a Zebra Technologies printer language)

As of 2009 other proprietary languages like GDI or SPL (Samsung Printer Language) are supported by Splix, a raster to SPL translator.[26]

However, several other alternatives can integrate with CUPS. Easy Software Products (ESP), the creators of CUPS, have released their own CUPS filters; Gutenprint (previously known as Gimp-Print) is a range of high-quality printer drivers for (mostly) inkjet printers, and TurboPrint for Linux has another range of quality printer drivers for a wide range of printers.

Backends

The backends are the ways in which CUPS sends data to printers. There are several backends available for CUPS: parallel, serial, and USB ports, as well as network backends that operate via the IPP, JetDirect (AppSocket), Line Printer Daemon ("LPD") and SMB protocols.

Compatibility

CUPS provides both the System V and Berkeley printing commands, so users can continue with traditional commands for printing via CUPS. CUPS listens on port 631, which is the standard IPP port, and optionally on port 515 by inetd, launchd, the Solaris Service Management Facility, or xinetd which use the cups-lpd helper program to support LPD printing. When CUPS is installed the lp System V printing system command and the lpr Berkeley printing system commands are installed as compatible programs. This allows a standard interface to CUPS and allows maximum compatibility with existing applications that rely on these printing systems.

User interface tools

Several tools exist to help set up CUPS.

CUPS web-based administration interface

CUPS has a web-based administration interface that runs on port 631.[27] It particularly helps organisations that need to monitor print jobs and add print queues and printers remotely.

CUPS 1.0 provided a simple class, job, and printer-monitoring interface for web browsers.

CUPS 1.1 replaced this interface with an enhanced administration interface that allows users to add, modify, delete, configure, and control classes, jobs, and printers.

CUPS 1.2 and later provide a revamped web interface which features improved readability and design, support for automatically discovered printers, and a better access to system logs and advanced settings.

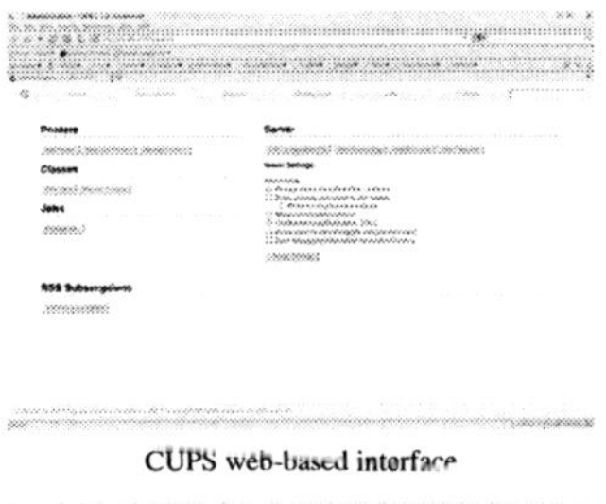

CUPS web-based interface

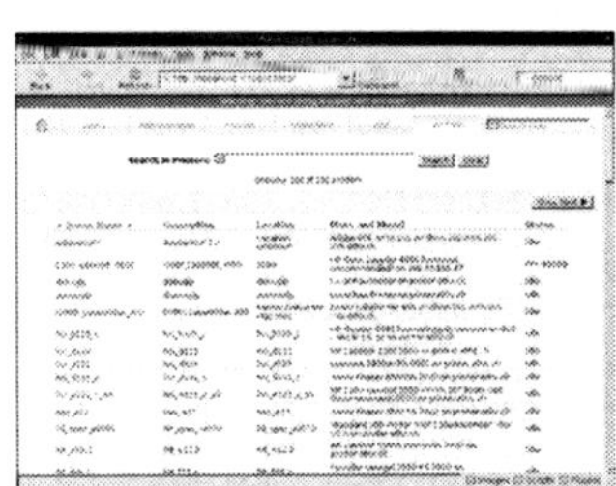

New CUPS web-based interface

GNOME

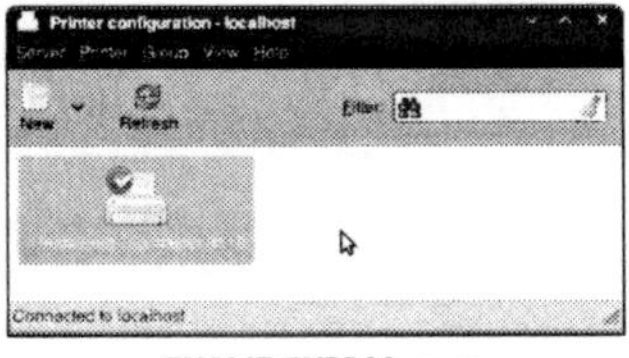

GNOME CUPS Manager

The GNOME CUPS Manager can add new CUPS printers and manage CUPS printers and queues. There are other third-party applications to manage printing, for example GtkLP [28] and its associate tool GtkLPQ, or GtkPSproc [29].

GNOME's widget toolkit GTK+ included integrated printing support based on CUPS in its version 2.10, released in 2006.

KDE

The KDEPrint framework for KDE contains various GUI-tools that act as CUPS front-ends and allows the administration of classes, print queues and print jobs; it includes a printer wizard to assist with adding new printers amongst other features.[30] KDEPrint first appeared in KDE 2.2.

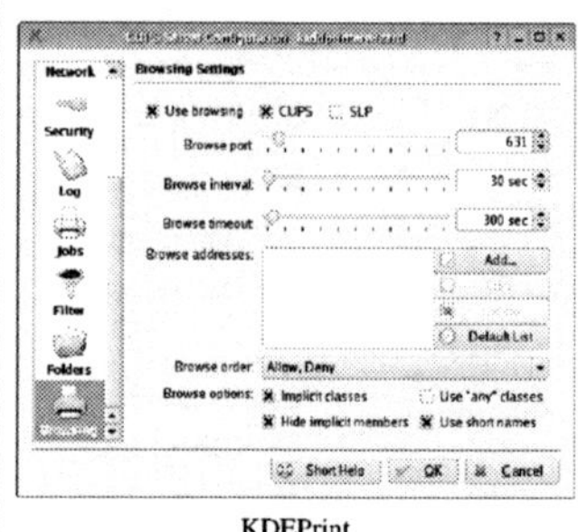

KDEPrint

KDEPrint supports several different printing platforms, with CUPS one of the best-supported. It replaced a previous version of printing support in KDE, *qtcups* and is backwards compatible with this module of KDE. As of 2009 *kprinter*, a dialogue-box program, serves as the main tool for sending jobs to the print device; it can also be started from the command line. KDEPrint includes a system to pre-filter any jobs before they are handed over to CUPS, or to handle jobs all on itself, such as converting files to PDF. These filters are described by a pair of Desktop/XML files.

KDEPrint's main components include:

- a Print Dialog box, which allows printer properties to be modified
- a Print Manager, which allows management of printers, such as adding and removing printers, through an Add Printer Wizard
- a Job Viewer/Manager, which manages printer jobs, such as hold/release, cancel and move to another printer
- a CUPS configuration module (integrated into KDE)

Mac OS X

In Mac OS X 10.5, printers are configured in the Print & Fax pane in System Preferences, and in printer proxy applications which display the print queues and allow additional configuration after printers are set up. Earlier versions of Mac OS X also included a Printer Setup Utility, which supplied configuration options missing from earlier versions of the Print & Fax preference pane.

Mandriva Linux

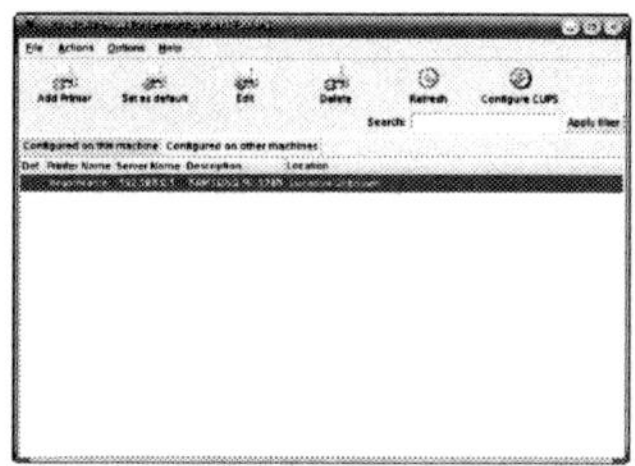

Mandriva Linux 10.1 up to version 2008.1 features a GUI for printing (Printerdrake). It is basically an interface for CUPS and allows users to add, remove and update printers, as well as the control of print jobs. This is done from a centralised configuration program that allows for CUPS server configuration in a centralised set of screens. As of 2009 it uses the Red Hat Enterprise Linux/Fedora printer frontend, called system-config-printer.

PrinterSetup

The PrinterSetup system can manage CUPS queues. It takes the approach of assigning a text file to describe each print queue. These 'PrinterSetupFiles' may then be added to other text files called 'PrinterSetupLists'. This allows logical grouping of printers. As of 2009 the PrinterSetup project remains in its infancy.[31]

Red Hat Linux/Fedora

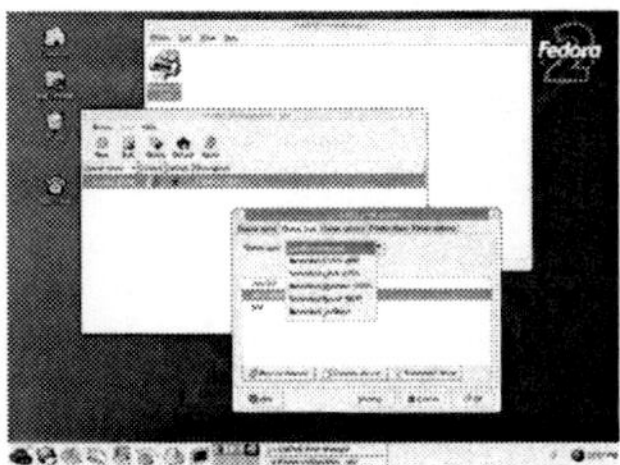
Fedora provides a print manager that can modify CUPS-based printers

Starting with Red Hat Linux 9, Red Hat provided an integrated print manager based on CUPS and integrated into GNOME. This allowed adding printers via a user interface similar to the one Microsoft Windows uses, where a new printer could be added using an *add new printer wizard*, along with changing default printer-properties in a window containing a list of installed printers. Jobs could also be started and stopped using a print manager and the printer could be paused using a context menu that pops up when the printer icon is right-clicked.

Eric Raymond criticised this system in his piece *The Luxury of Ignorance*. Raymond had attempted to install CUPS using the Fedora Core 1 print manager but found it non-intuitive; he criticised the interface designers for not designing with the user's point-of-view in mind. He found the idea of printer queues was not obvious because users create queues on their local computer but these queues are actually created on the CUPS server.

He also found the plethora of queue type options confusing as he could choose from between networked CUPS (IPP), networked Unix (LPD), networked Windows (SMB), networked Novell (NCP) or networked JetDirect. He found the help file singularly unhelpful and largely irrelevant to a user's needs. Raymond used CUPS as a general topic to show that user interface design on Linux desktops needs rethinking and more careful design. He stated:[32]

> The meta-problem here is that the configuration wizard does all the approved rituals (GUI with standardized clicky buttons, help popping up in a browser, etc. etc.) but doesn't have the central attribute these are supposed to achieve: discoverability. That is, the quality that every point in the interface has prompts and actions attached to it from which you can learn what to do next. Does your project have this quality?

ESP Print Pro

Easy Software Products, the original creators of CUPS, created a GUI, provided support for many printers and implemented a PostScript RIP. ESP Print Pro ran on Windows, UNIX and Linux, but is no longer available and support for it ended on 31 December 2007.[33]

See also

- Foomatic
- Gutenprint
- LPRng
- Scanner Access Now Easy
- Spooling
- Xprint

Notes and references

[1] CUPS Software License Agreement (http://www.cups.org/documentation.php/doc-1.4/license.html), see section "License Exceptions". Last accessed July 10, 2009

[2] Michael Sweet (June 9, 1999), "A Bright New Future for Printing on Linux" (http://linuxtoday.com/news_story.php3?ltsn=1999-06-09-014-10-NW-SM), *Linux Today* & followup from Michael Sweet (June 11, 1999), "The Future Brightens for Linux Printing" (http://linuxtoday.com/news_story.php3?ltsn=1999-06-11-018-10-NW-SM), *Linux Today*.

[3] *Easy Software Products*, CUPS Licensed for Use in Apple Operating Systems! (http://www.cups.org/articles.php?L68+I10+T+P1+Qapple) (press release), March 1, 2002.

[4] "CUPS", CUPS Purchased by Apple Inc. (http://www.cups.org/articles.php?L475) (press release), July 11, 2007.

[5] *Easy Software Products*, CUPS Design Description (http://www.cups.org/documentation.php/spec-design.html), see section "Scheduler". Last accessed January 9, 2007

[6] *Easy Software Products*, CUPS Design Description (http://www.cups.org/documentation.php/spec-design.html), see section "Filters". Last accessed January 9th, 2007

[7] *Easy Software Products*, CUPS Design Description (http://www.cups.org/documentation.php/spec-design.html), see section "Backend". Last accessed January 9, 2007

[8] *Easy Software Products*. CUPS Software Design, Authorization (http://www.cups.org/doc-1.1/sdd.html#3_8_1). Last accessed January 9, 2007.

[9] *Easy Software Products*. CUPS Software Administrators Manual, Authorisation (http://www.cups.org/doc-1.1/sdd.html#3_8_3). Last accessed January 9th, 2007.

[10] *Easy Software Products*. CUPS Software Design, IPP (http://www.cups.org/doc-1.1/sdd.html#3_8_7). Last accessed January 9, 2007.

[11] *Easy Software Products*. CUPS Software Administrators Manual, Classes (http://www.cups.org/doc-1.1/sam.html#2_4). Last accessed January 9, 2007.

[12] *Easy Software Products*. CUPS Software Administrators Manual, Jobs (http://www.cups.org/doc-1.1/sam.html#2_3). Last accessed January 9th, 2007.

[13] *Easy Software Products*. CUPS Software Design, Configuration (http://www.cups.org/doc-1.1/sdd.html#3_8_4). Last accessed January 9, 2007.

[14] *Easy Software Products*. CUPS Software Design, Logging (http://www.cups.org/doc-1.1/sdd.html#3_8_9). Last accessed January 9, 2007.

[15] *Easy Software Products*. CUPS Software Design, MIME (http://www.cups.org/doc-1.1/sdd.html#3_8_11). Last accessed January 9, 2007.

[16] *Easy Software Products*. CUPS Software Design, PPD (http://www.cups.org/doc-1.1/sdd.html#3_8_12). Last accessed January 9, 2007.

[17] *Easy Software Products*. CUPS Software Design, Devices (http://www.cups.org/doc-1.1/sdd.html#3_8_5). Last accessed January 9, 2007.

[18] *Easy Software Products*. CUPS Software Design, Printers (http://www.cups.org/doc-1.1/sdd.html#3_8_13). Last accessed January 9th, 2007.

[19] *Easy Software Products*. CUPS Software Administrators Manual, Filters (http://www.cups.org/doc-1.1/sam.html#2_5). Last accessed January 9, 2007.

[20] *Easy Software Products*. CUPS Software Design, Filters (http://www.cups.org/doc-1.1/sdd.html#3_7). Last accessed January 9th, 2007.

[21] *Easy Software Products*. CUPS Software Administrators Manual, File Typing and Filtering (http://www.cups.org/doc-1.1/sam.html#FILE_TYPING_FILTERING). Last accessed January 9, 2007.

[22] *Easy Software Products*. CUPS Software Administrators Manual, mime.types (http://www.cups.org/doc-1.1/sam.html#7_13_1). Last accessed January 9th, 2007.

[23] *Easy Software Products*. CUPS Software Administrators Manual, mime.convs (http://www.cups.org/doc-1.1/sam.html#7_13_é). Last accessed January 9, 2007.

[24] *Easy Software Products*. CUPS Software Administrators Manual, pstops (http://www.cups.org/doc-1.1/sdd.html#3_7_5). Last accessed January 9, 2007.

[25] The MIME type for the CUPS raster format is application/vnd.cups-raster.

[26] Aplix home page (http://splix.ap2c.org/)

[27] CUPS Software Administrators Manual (http://www.cups.org/sam.html#4_4), "Managing Printers from the Web"

[28] http://gtklp.sourceforge.net

[29] http://www.rastersoft.com/gtkpsproc.html

[30] printing.kde.org Webmaster (undated). "KDEPrint Homepage" (http://printing.kde.org/). . Retrieved 2008-04-02.

[31] Printer Setup is in a prototyping phase (http://www.lucidsystems.org/printersetup/moreinformation.php), *Lucid Information Systems*

[32] "The Luxury of Ignorance: An Open-Source Horror Story" (http://www.catb.org/~esr/writings/cups-horror.html)

[33] Easy Software Products' ESP Print Pro (http://www.easysw.com/discontinued.php)

- Sweet, Michael (July 10, 2000). CUPS overview (http://www.cups.org/overview.html). *Easy Software Products*.

- CUPS software administration manual : Managing printers from the web (http://www.cups.org/sam.html#4_4) (version 1.1.21, 2004). *Easy Software Products*. Retrieved January 5, 2005.
- http://www.cups.org/articles.php How-to articles and FAQs about using CUPS
- Design of CUPS Filtering System — including the context for Mac OS X ("Jaguar") (http://www.linuxprinting.org/CUPS-Filter-Chart.html). *LinuxPrinting.org*. Retrieved January 5, 2005.
- KDE. *KDEPrint information* (http://printing.kde.org/info/). KDE-printing website. Retrieved January 14, 2005.

External links

- Official website (http://www.cups.org/)
- CUPS (http://freshmeat.net/projects/cups/) at Freshmeat
- OpenPrinting (http://www.linux-foundation.org/en/OpenPrinting)
- Universal Plug and Play - Printer Device V 1.0 and Printer Basic Service V 1.0 (http://www.upnp.org/standardizeddcps/printer.asp)

DOCS (software)

DOCS, Display Operator Console Support, was a systems software package that provided video display for the IBM/370 running DOS/VS and DOS/VSE environments, and IBM/360 retrofitted with modified DOS, such as TCSC's EDOS.

The product

Computer operators communicated with IBM mainframe computers using an electro-mechanical typewriter-like console that came standard on most IBM 360 and 370 computer, except a few upper end models that offered video consoles and the Model 20 which came standard without a console.

The majority of smaller and less expensive IBM 360s and 370s came equipped with these ruggedized Selectric keyboard devices. The Selectric was a major step up from the teletypes (TTY) associated with Unix and smaller systems, but still clunky. The video consoles provided with certain models were not considered particularly user friendly, and they ignored two thirds of IBM's mainframe market, DOS and its VSE descendants.

DOCS replaced or supplanted the typewriter interface with a video screen. In practice, it worked a little like present-day instant messenger programs (ICQ, QQ, AIM, Adium, iChat, etc), with a data entry line at the bottom and messages scrolling in real time up the screen. The commands were otherwise identical.

DOCS was available for DOS, DOS/VS, DOS/VSE, and came packaged with third party operating systems, such as EDOS from The Computer Software Company, later acquired by Nixdorf.

Platforms

Software

The product ran under several DOS-related platforms:

- DOS/VS
- DOS/VSE
- DOS, modified
- EDOS
- vDOS

Hardware

Several venders offered DOCS as part of their OS:

- Amdahl
- Fujitsu
- Hitachi
- Magnuson
- RCA

Development

DOCS was developed by CFS, Inc. of Brookline, Massachusetts at the Kayser-Roth data center in Whitman, Massachusetts. Dick Goran wrote the video interface. Leigh Lundin wrote the operating system interface and transcript recorder.

Fx

DOCS required a dedicated partition. With DOS having only three partitions and DOS/VS seven, giving up a partition to DOCS placed a crimp in practicability.

Leigh Lundin designed **Fx**, a pseudo-partition that relieved the user from relinquishing a working partition. Fx appeared in the DOS/VS version of SDI's Grasp as F0.

Marketing

DOCS was sold in North America by CFS, Inc, Brookline, Ma.

For overseas sales, CFS engaged in both mail order and local vendors. The product was also embedded in third party operating system packages, such as EDOS and vDOS.

DirectX Video Acceleration

DirectX Video Acceleration (**DXVA**) is a Microsoft API specification for the Microsoft Windows and Xbox 360 platforms that allows video decoding to be hardware accelerated. The pipeline allows certain CPU-intensive operations such as iDCT, motion compensation and deinterlacing to be offloaded to the GPU. DXVA 2.0 allows more operations, including video capturing and processing operations, to be hardware accelerated as well.

DXVA works in conjunction with the video rendering model used by the video card. DXVA 1.0, which was introduced as a standardized API with Windows 2000 and is currently available on Windows 98 or later, can use either the overlay rendering mode or VMR 7/9.[1] DXVA 2.0, available only on Windows Vista, Windows 7 and later OSs, integrates with Media Foundation (MF) and uses the Enhanced Video Renderer (EVR) present in MF.[1]

Overview

The DXVA is used by software video decoders to define a codec-specific pipeline for hardware-accelerated decoding and rendering of the codec. The pipeline starts at the CPU which is used for parsing the media stream and conversion to DXVA-compatible structures. DXVA specifies a set of operations that can be hardware accelerated and device driver interfaces (DDIs) that the graphic driver can implement to accelerate the operations. If the codec needs any of the supported operations, it can use these interfaces to access the hardware-accelerated implementation of these operations. If the graphic driver does not implement one or more of the interfaces, it is up to the codec to provide a software fallback for it. The decoded video is handed over to the hardware video renderer where further video post-processing might be applied to it before being rendered to the device. The resulting pipeline is usable in a DirectShow compatible application.

DXVA specifies the Motion Compensation DDI, which specifies the interfaces for iDCT operations, Huffman coding, motion compensation, alpha blending, inverse quantization, color space conversion and frame-rate conversion operations, among others.[2] [3] It also includes three sub-specifications: Deinterlacing DDI, COPP DDI and ProcAmp DDI.[4] The Deinterlacing DDI specifies the callbacks for deinterlacing operations. The COPP (Certified Output Protection Protocol) DDI functions allow the pipeline to be secured for DRM-protected media, by specifying encryption functions. The ProcAmp DDI is used to accelerate post-processing video. The ProcAmp driver module sits between the hardware video renderer and the display driver and provides functions for applying post-processing filters on the decompressed video.

The functions exposed by DXVA DDIs are not accessible directly by a DirectShow client, but are supplied as callback functions to the video renderer. As such, the renderer plays a very important role in anchoring the pipeline.

DXVA on Windows Vista and later

DXVA 2.0 enhances the implementation of the video pipeline and adds a host of other DDIs, including a Capture DDI for video capture. The DDIs it shares with DXVA 1.0 are also enhanced with support for hardware acceleration of more operations. Also, the DDI functions are directly available to callers and need not be mediated by the video renderer.[5] As such, pipelines for simply decoding the media (without rendering) or post-processing and rendering (without decoding) can also be created. These features require the Windows Display Driver Model drivers, which limit DXVA 2.0 to Windows Vista, Windows Server 2008[5] [1] , Windows 7 and Windows Server 2008 R2. DXVA 2.0 supports only Enhanced Video Renderer as the video renderer on Vista & Windows 7(with XP, DXVA-Rendering is possible with VMR9 and the well-known Overlay Mixer).[1] DXVA integrates with Media Foundation and allows DXVA pipelines to be exposed as *Media Foundation Transforms* (*MFTs*). Even decoder pipelines or post-processing pipelines can be exposed as MFTs, which can be used by the Media Foundation topology loader to create a full media playback pipeline. DXVA 1.0 is emulated using DXVA 2.0.[1] DXVA 2.0 does not include the COPP DDI, rather it uses PVP for protected content. For Windows XP and Windows 2000 DXVA

1.0 can be used. Windows 7 supports DXVA-HD [6] if WDDM 1.1 is supported.

Software support

- Media Player Classic Home Cinema
- Adobe Flash version 10.1
- Boxee
- XBMC (Dsplayer Branch and nightly builds)
- MediaPortal
- Microsoft Windows Vista/Windows 7 internal MPEG-2 decoder
- Nero Showtime
- Nero MediaHub
- PowerDVD
- SPlayer[7]
- WinDVD
- Windows Media Player 11 (WMV only)
- Windows Media Player 12
- Ffdshow (Since Revision 3185)
- Anysee Viewer
- DivX H.264 Decoder (version 1.2, part of the DivX Plus software)
- VLC media player (DXVA 2.0 only)[8] (since version 1.1)

See also

- Nvidia PureVideo - the bit-stream technology from NVIDIA used in their graphics chips to accelerate video decoding on hardware GPU with DXVA.
- UVD (Unified Video Decoder) - is the video decoding bit-stream technology from ATI Technologies to support hardware (GPU) decode with DXVA.
- Media Foundation (and its Enhanced Video Renderer) which DXVA 2.0 uses.
- VDPAU (Video Decode and Presentation API for Unix)
- X-Video Bitstream Acceleration (XvBA), the X11 equivalent of DXVA for MPEG-2, H.264, and VC-1
- X-Video Motion Compensation, the X11 equivalent for MPEG-2 video codec only
- Video Acceleration API (VAAPI)
- Video Decode Acceleration Framework is Apple Inc.s API for hardware-accelerated decoding of H.264 on Mac OS X

External links

- DirectX Video Acceleration [9]
- DXVAChecker [10], utility listing supported DXVA modes on the given computer
- DivX DXVA guide [11], walk-through of checking for DXVA support and enabling it in the DivX H.264 Decoder

References

[1] "DirectX Video Acceleration 2.0" (http://msdn2.microsoft.com/en-us/library/aa965263.aspx). . Retrieved 2007-10-24.
[2] "Introduction to DirectX VA" (http://msdn2.microsoft.com/en-us/library/ms799545.aspx). . Retrieved 2007-10-24.
[3] "Microsoft DirectX Video Acceleration (DirectX VA) support" (http://forum.videolan.org/viewtopic.php?t=9421). . Retrieved 2007-10-24.
[4] "DirectX Video Acceleration" (http://msdn2.microsoft.com/en-us/library/ms798379.aspx). . Retrieved 2007-10-24.
[5] "What's New in DirectShow" (http://msdn2.microsoft.com/en-us/library/ms788119.aspx). . Retrieved 2007-10-24.
[6] DXVA-HD (http://msdn.microsoft.com/en-us/library/ee663586(VS.85).aspx)

[7] http://splayer.org
[8] http://wiki.videolan.org/VLC_DxVA2
[9] http://msdn2.microsoft.com/en-us/library/ms798379.aspx
[10] http://bluesky23.hp.infoseek.co.jp/en/index.html#DXVAChecker
[11] http://labs.divx.com/DivX-H264-Decoder-DXVA

Driver Verifier

Driver Verifier
A component of Microsoft Windows

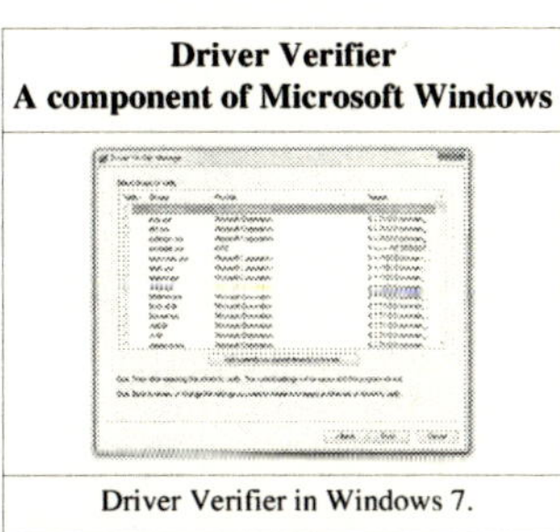

Driver Verifier in Windows 7.

Driver Verifier is a tool included in Microsoft Windows that replaces the default operating system subroutines with ones that are specifically developed to catch device driver bugs. [1] Once enabled, it monitors and stresses drivers to detect illegal function calls or actions that may be causing system corruption. It acts within the kernel mode and can target specific device drivers for continual checking or make driver verifier functionality multithreaded, so that several device drivers can be monitored at the same time. [1] It can simulate certain conditions such as low memory, I/O verification, pool tracking, IRQL checking, deadlock detection, DMA checks, IRP logging etc.[1]

Driver Verifier (Verifier.exe) was first introduced as a command-line utility in Windows 2000 [1] ; in Windows XP, it gained an easy to use graphical user interface, called *Driver Verifier Manager* using which it is possible to enable a standard or custom set of settings to select which drivers to test and verify. Each new Windows version has since introduced several new, more stringent checks for testing and verifying drivers and detecting new classes of driver defects.

Driver Verifier should be enabled with caution on production systems as it can expose and enable undetected bugs in drivers, especially ones which are not digitally signed by Windows Hardware Quality Labs, causing the system to display blue screen errors. Microsoft recommends not all drivers should be verified at the same time. [2]

External links

- Driver Verifier Homepage on WHDC [3]

References

[1] How Windows XP's Device Driver Verifier Works (http://www.informit.com/articles/printerfriendly.aspx?p=22085)
[2] Things to consider before you enable Driver Verifier Manager on production servers (http://support.microsoft.com/kb/251233)
[3] http://www.microsoft.com/whdc/DevTools/tools/DrvVerifier.mspx

F6 disk

F6 disk is a colloquial name for a floppy disk containing a Microsoft Windows NT device driver for a SCSI or RAID system. F6 disks are used by other NT-based versions of Windows, including Windows 2000, Windows Server 2003, and Windows XP. On Windows Vista, F6 disks are obsolete; its setup process supports loading third-party drivers from CD-ROMs and USB drives.

Usage

An F6 disk is named after the manner in which it is used. During the installation process for Windows, the Setup program must load device drivers for the disk system on which Windows will be installed. Unless the disk system has been established on the market before the finalization of the particular Windows release, the drivers are not included on the Windows installation discs, and must be loaded by means of an F6 disk. An F6 disk is loaded in Windows setup by pressing the F6 key immediately when Windows Setup starts. The message "Press F6 if you need to install a third party SCSI or RAID driver..." is briefly flashed on the screen every time Windows Setup starts.

An F6 disk contains device drivers in its root directory. F6 disks are always floppy disks - the device drivers loaded by Windows Setup at the point of the F6 prompt are unable to read any media other than floppies, with the exception of Windows Vista, which adds USB-flash-memory support or fixed disk support for this situation. Device drivers for RAID and other disk controllers are often provided on CD-ROM, but must be copied to a floppy F6 disk if they are to be used during Windows Setup. An alternate approach to this particular problem is slipstreaming of the required SATA/SCSI/SAS/RAID/EIDE drivers into the windows installation files directory (e.g. i386 for the x86 variety) by means of software like nLite, and create an ISO image that can be burned to CD or DVD media.

References

- Microsoft support, KB313348 [1]

References

[1] http://support.microsoft.com/?kbid=313348

FreedomHEC

FreedomHEC (a play on WinHEC) is an annual "unconference" for computer hardware engineers and device driver developers. FreedomHEC focuses on making computer hardware interoperate with free software and open source operating systems, especially Linux.

The first FreedomHEC conference was held May 26–27, 2006, in Seattle. The second was held May 18–19, 2007 in Los Angeles. FreedomHEC is scheduled immediately before or after WinHEC—and in the same city—so that developers who want to attend both need only make one trip.

External links

- Official website [1]
- FreedomHEC 2007 wiki [2]

References

[1] http://freedomhec.org/
[2] http://freedomhec.pbwiki.com/

HostAP

Developer(s)	Jouni Malinen & others
Stable release	0.6.9 / March 23, 2009
Operating system	Linux
Type	WLAN device drivers
License	GPLv2
Website	hostap.epitest.fi [1]

HostAP is one of the most popular IEEE 802.11 device drivers for Linux. It works with cards using the Conexant (formerly Intersil) Prism 2/2.5/3 chipset and support Host AP mode, which allows a WLAN card to perform all the functions of an access point.

The driver code was written by Jouni Malinen, hired by Atheros in 2008 [2] , and was included into the main kernel tree in Linux 2.6.14

See also

- Hostapd
- wpa supplicant
- Intel PRO/Wireless 2200BG AP Driver [3] for Linux, an open source 802.11 b/g access point driver for the ipw2200 and ipw2915

External links

- HostAP Homepage [1]

References

[1] http://hostap.epitest.fi/
[2] http://madwifi-project.org/wiki/news/20080725/ath9k-atheros-unveils-free-linux-driver-for
[3] http://sourceforge.net/projects/ipw2200-ap

I/O request packet

I/O request packets (IRPs) are kernel mode structures that are used by Windows Driver Model (WDM) and Windows NT device drivers to communicate with each other and with the operating system. They are data structures that describe I/O requests, and can be equally well thought of as "I/O request descriptors" or similar. Rather than passing a large number of small arguments (such as buffer address, buffer size, I/O function type, etc.) to a driver, all of these parameters are passed via a single pointer to this persistent data structure. The IRP with all of its parameters can be put on a queue if the I/O request cannot be performed immediately. I/O completion is reported back to the I/O manager by passing its address to a routine for that purpose, IoCompleteRequest. The IRP may be repurposed as a special kernel APC object if such is required to report completion of the I/O to the requesting thread.

IRPs are typically created by the I/O Manager in response to I/O requests from user mode. However, IRPs are sometimes created by the plug-and-play manager, power manager, and other system components, and can also be created by drivers and then passed to other drivers.

The I/O request packet mechanism is also used by the VMS operating system, and was used by Digital's RSX family of operating systems before that.

See also

- Architecture of Windows NT

References and external links

- Whitepaper on Windows I/O model [1]
- How Device Drivers work [2]

References

[1] http://www.microsoft.com/technet/archive/winntas/training/ntarchitectoview/ntarc_6.mspx?mfr=true
[2] http://technet2.microsoft.com/windowsserver/en/library/2e81a334-ece5-4210-815a-6a2ea33f61151033.mspx?mfr=true

IA-32 Execution Layer

Original author(s)	Intel
Stable release	5336 / 5.3.81.31.21
Operating system	Linux, Windows Server
Type	Emulator
License	LGPL, Proprietary

The **IA-32 Execution Layer** (IA-32 EL) is a software emulator in the form of a software driver that improves performance of 32-bit applications running on 64-bit Intel Itanium-based systems, particularly those running Linux and Windows Server 2003 (it is included in Windows 2003 SP1 and later[1] and in most Linux distributions for Itanium). The IA-32 EL bypasses the slow x86 hardware emulation which is available on pre-Montecito Itanium models.

Part of the software is under the LGPL and part is under an Intel proprietary license.[2]

References

[1] The IA-32 Execution Layer 4.3 Software Driver (http://www.microsoft.com/windowsserver2003/64bit/ipf/ia32el.mspx) (microsoft.com)

[2] Intel Software Development Products (http://www.intel.com/cd/software/products/asmo-na/eng/219740.htm) (download page)

- IA-32 EL Linux link from Intel (http://www.intel.com/cd/software/products/asmo-na/eng/219773.htm) dead link

J/XFS

J/XFS is an alternative API to CEN/XFS (which is Windows specific) and also to Xpeak (which is Operating System independent, based on XML messages). J/XFS is written in Java with the objective to provide a platform agnostic client-server architecture for financial applications, especially peripheral devices such as EFTPOS terminals and ATMs which are unique to the financial industry.

With the move to a more standardized software base, financial institutions have been increasingly interested in the ability to pick and choose the application programs that drive their equipment. J/XFS provides a common Object Oriented API between a pure Java application and a wide range of financial devices, providing a layer of separation between application and device logic that can be implemented using a native J/XFS API or wrapping an existing implementation in JavaPOS or CEN/XFS.

J/XFS was developed by leading system suppliers DeLaRue, IBM, NCR, Wincor Nixdorf and Sun Microsystems and is now hosted, monitored and maintained by the European Committee for Standardisation, CEN.

History

Chronology:

- 1998 - The J/XFS Forum founded with initial meeting held in Stuttgart, Germany. Host: IBM.
- 1999 - First meetings, introduction of J/XFS to the CEN standardisation body in Brussels, Belgium, and release 1.0.
- 2000 - Release of FDI 1.01.
- 2001 - Releases of FDI 1.1, 2.0 and 2.1.
- 2002 - Next version of J/XFS due for release.
- 2004 - Publication of new J/XFS CEN Standard Version CWA 14329.

Devices covered by the specifications

- Printer Devices
- Receipt/Journal/Passbook/Document-Printer and Scanner
- Cash Dispenser/Recycler
- Pin Pad Device
- ID Card
- Chip Card and Magnetic Stripe Devices
- Text I/O Device
- Alarm Device
- Depository Units
- Check Readers and Scanners
- Sensors and Indicators
- Cameras

External links

- J/XFS Home Page [1]
- CEN Workshop J/XFS [2]
- Xpeak Home Page [3]

References

[1] http://jxfs.net/
[2] http://www.cen.eu/cenorm/sectors/sectors/isss/activity/wsjxfs.asp
[3] http://www.xpeak.org/

Kernel-Mode Driver Framework

The **Kernel-Mode Driver Framework** (KMDF) is a driver framework developed by Microsoft as a tool to aid driver developers create and maintain Kernel mode device drivers for Windows 2000[1] and later releases. It is one of the frameworks included in the Windows Driver Foundation. The current version is 1.9.

Relationship to WDM

In general, KMDF supports drivers that were written for the Windows Driver Model, and it runs on WDM. WDM is the driver model used since the advent of Windows 98, whereas KMDF is the driver framework Microsoft advocates and uses for Windows 2000 and beyond.

In general, since more features like power management and plug and play are handled by the framework, a KMDF driver is less complicated and has less code than an equivalent WDM driver.

KMDF is object-based, built on top of WDM. It provides an object-based perspective to WDM, following the architectural mandate of its superset, WDF. The functionality is contained in different types of objects. KMDF implementation consists of:

- plug and play and power management
- I/O queues
- Direct memory access (DMA)
- Windows Management Instrumentation (WMI)
- Synchronization

See also

- Windows Driver Foundation
- User-Mode Driver Framework
- Windows Driver Model
- Windows Vista

References

- Windows Driver Kit [2]
- Kernel-Mode Driver Framework Homepage [3]
- Microsoft KMDF Paper [4]

References

[1] . The original release of KMDF only supported Windows XP and Server 2003. Support for Windows 2000 was added in KMDF version 1.1.
[2] http://www.microsoft.com/whdc/devtools/WDK/default.mspx
[3] http://www.microsoft.com/whdc/driver/wdf/KMDF.mspx
[4] http://download.microsoft.com/download/9/c/5/9c5b2167-8017-4bae-9fde-d599bac8184a/KMDF-arch.doc#_Toc120013745

Leaf driver

Leaf driver refers to a device driver that accesses logically or physically existent devices on an I/O bus, and implements the functions defined for the device, such as transferring data to or from the device or accessing device registers.

Leaf devices (those requiring leaf drivers) are typical peripheral devices such as disks, tapes, network adapters, frame buffers, and so forth. Drivers for these devices export the traditional character and block driver interfaces for use by user processes to read and write data to storage or communication devices.

See also Nexus driver.

Mirror driver

A **mirror driver** is a display driver for a virtual device that mirrors the drawing operations of one or more additional physical display devices.

When video mirroring is active, each time the system draws to the primary video device at a location inside the mirrored area, a copy of the draw operation is executed on the mirrored video device in real-time.[1]

Mirror drivers are based on the Windows XP display driver model. The new Desktop Window Manager in Windows Vista is using the Windows Vista Windows Display Driver Model that is not supported by mirror drivers technology. Therefore, while a mirror driver is active, Windows disables Desktop Window Manager and Windows Aero. [2]

Mirror driver is used in screen readers such as JAWS, Window-Eyes and FreedomBox; the monitoring software LanSchool; and remote desktop software such as LogMeIn, UltraVNC, TightVNC and Radmin.

External links

- MSDN Library - Mirror Drivers article [3]

References

[1] "Windows Driver Kit: Glossary" (http://msdn2.microsoft.com/en-us/library/ms789543.aspx). Microsoft Developer Network. .
[2] Campbell, Matt; Calvo, Mike (2008-03-21). "The Facts About Mirror Drivers in Assistive Technology" (http://serotek.com/mirror-driver-paper.html) (– Scholar search (http://scholar.google.co.uk/scholar?hl=en&lr=&q=intitle:The+Facts+About+Mirror+Drivers+in+Assistive+Technology&as_publication=&as_ylo=&as_yhi=&btnG=Search)). . Retrieved 2008-04-24
[3] http://msdn2.microsoft.com/en-us/library/ms797878.aspx

Mode-setting

Mode-setting is setting up the screen resolution and depth mode for the graphics card. Modern mode setting software support multiple monitors ("multi-head") and hot plugging.

Location

Mode-setting can be done in kernel space or in user space. Doing mode-setting in kernel-space is more flexible. Doing kernel-based mode-setting allows displaying an error in the case of a fatal error in the kernel, even when using a user-space display server. User-space mode-setting would have needed superuser privileges for direct hardware access. So kernel-based mode-setting increases security because the user-space graphics server does not need superuser privileges.

Implementations

Microsoft Windows

Microsoft Windows versions that are NT-based use kernel mode setting. The kernel error display made possible by kernel mode setting is known as the Blue Screen of Death.

Linux

The Linux kernel got the prerequisite for kernel-based mode-setting by accepting Graphics Execution Manager (GEM) in version 2.6.28,[1] released December 2008. This will be replaced by a TTM (Translation Table Maps) memory manager which supports the GEM API.[2] TTM was developed for the ATI Radeon driver and VIA S3 Graphics chipsets.[3]

Support for Intel GMA graphic cards has been accepted in version 2.6.29 which was released on March 23, 2009.[4]

Support for pre-R600 ATI Radeon graphics cards has been accepted in version 2.6.31 which was released on September 9, 2009.[5] Support for R600 and R700 was in development within DRM and has been merged in version 2.6.32.[6] Support for Evergreen (R800) has been merged in version 2.6.34.

As NVIDIA did not release all the needed documentation for its graphics chip, the development is under the nouveau project which uses reverse engineering to get it to work. Nouveau has been pulled to 2.6.33 kernel. This will allow to use kernel-based mode-setting for NVIDIA cards with this driver.

OpenBSD

OpenBSD which has a strong focus on security is interested to get kernel-based mode-setting in order to run X without superuser privileges.[7]

OpenSolaris

OpenSolaris will feature kernel-based mode-setting.[8] OpenSolaris also has GEM support as of snv_130.

See also

- Screens of death
- Blue Screen of Death
- Black Screen of Death

External links

- http://www.x.org/wiki/ModeSetting
- http://www.x.org/wiki/IntelGraphicsDriver – Intel driver
- http://www.x.org/wiki/RadeonFeature – ATI Radeon driver
- http://nouveau.freedesktop.org/wiki/ – NVIDIA driver (nouveau)
- http://fedoraproject.org/wiki/Features/KernelModesetting

References

[1] http://kernelnewbies.org/Linux_2_6_28#head-b957b19f6139b6bbbfabaf790bf643b1746985d6
[2] http://www.phoronix.com/scan.php?page=news_item&px=NjY3Ng
[3] http://www.phoronix.com/scan.php?page=news_item&px=NzMxOA
[4] http://kernelnewbies.org/Linux_2_6_29#head-e1bab8dc862e3b477cc38d87e8ddc779a66509d1
[5] http://kernelnewbies.org/Linux_2_6_31#head-78158343fc06e5e289f2ccaf51d6a30090a46524
[6] http://www.phoronix.com/scan.php?page=article&item=amd_r600_r700_2d
[7] http://www.phoronix.com/scan.php?page=news_item&px=NzA5Mg
[8] http://www.phoronix.com/scan.php?page=news_item&px=NzIwMA

NDISwrapper

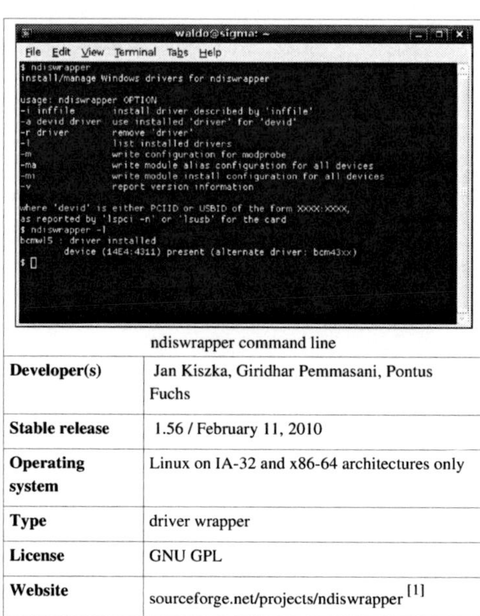

ndiswrapper command line

Developer(s)	Jan Kiszka, Giridhar Pemmasani, Pontus Fuchs
Stable release	1.56 / February 11, 2010
Operating system	Linux on IA-32 and x86-64 architectures only
Type	driver wrapper
License	GNU GPL
Website	sourceforge.net/projects/ndiswrapper [1]

NDISwrapper is a free software driver wrapper that enables the use of Windows XP drivers for network devices (cards, USB modems, and routers), on Unix-like operating systems, for devices sharing the same architecture only, namely either IA-32 or x86-64. NDISwrapper works by implementing the Windows kernel and NDIS APIs, and dynamically linking the driver to this implementation.

Native drivers for Unix and Linux are not available for some network adapters, as manufacturers supply neither drivers nor the information required to write them. NDISwrapper allows Windows drivers available for virtually all adapters to be used under Unix and Linux.

Use

NDISwrapper requires at least the ".inf" and the ".sys" files invariably supplied as parts of the Windows driver. For example, if the driver is called "mydriver", with the files mydriver.inf and mydriver.sys and vendorid:productid 0000:0000, then NDISwrapper installs the driver to /etc/ndiswrapper/mydriver/. This directory contains three files:

- 0000:0000.conf, which contains information extracted from the inf file
- mydriver.inf (the original inf file)
- mydriver.sys (the driver file)

Graphical frontends

There are graphical frontends to NDISwrapper, such as Ndisgtk and NdisConfig, which allow NDISwrapper to be installed using a graphical user interface rather than console commands.

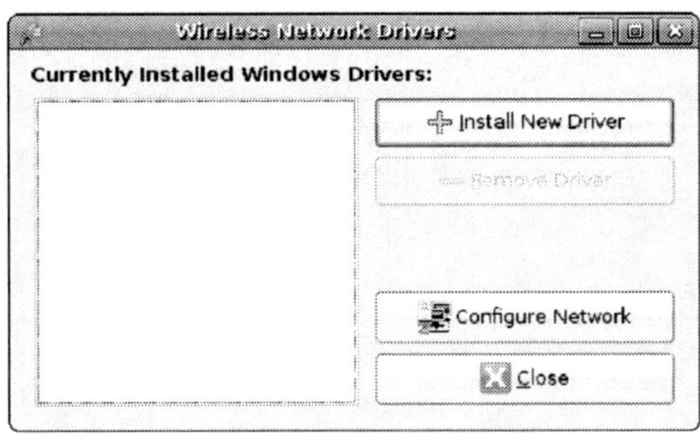

Ndisgtk graphical interface

Architecture

NDISwrapper enables a Linux system to use Windows drivers of type NDIS and WIFI. It was useful at a time where there was no Linux WIFI drivers for common WIFI cards. It works only on X86 computers because it uses Windows drivers which are only developed for X86 at the moment. It is composed of:

- A NDIS driver, which is a kind of overlay for Ethernet drivers.
- A WIFI manager, to control the radio and security part of the WIFI card.
- An USB manager and a PnP manager to make it possible to use WIFI card embedded in USB sticks.
- A minimal Ntoskrnl simulating the DDK for:
  - managing calls from the Windows driver.
  - managing IRP to the Windows driver (WDM only at the moment)
  - managing filter drivers in a simplistic way
  - loading/unloading Windows drivers
- A wrapper converting Linux calls to Windows and the other way round, also managing results and error codes

How it works

When a Linux application calls a device which is registered on Linux as a NDISwrapper device, the NDISwrapper determines which Windows driver is targeted. It then converts the Linux query in Windows parlance, it calls the Windows driver, wait for the result and translate it in Linux parlance then send back the result to the Linux application. It's possible from a Linux driver (NDISwrapper is a Linux driver) to call a Windows driver because they both execute in the same address space (the same as the Linux kernel). If the Windows driver is composed of layered drivers (for example one for Ethernet above one for USB) it's the upper layer driver which is called, and this upper layer will create new calls (IRP in Windows parlance) by calling the "mini ntoskrnl". So the "mini ntoskrnl" must know there are other drivers, it must have registered them in its internal database a priori by reading the Windows ".inf" files.

Similar programs

DriverLoader [2] is a commercial tool produced by Linuxant for Linux which seems to provide the same functionality as NDISwrapper.

Independently of but roughly simultaneously with the NDISwrapper project, Bill Paul of Wind River Systems developed a similar system, known as **Project Evil** or **The NDISulator**, for FreeBSD. It has since been ported to DragonFly BSD and NetBSD.

Limitations

The inability to use the drivers on other architectures such as PowerPC or Alpha is a limitation. Also, NDISwrapper does not implement NDIS 6 (Windows Vista version) yet, limiting drivers to Windows XP [3] . While it is not a major problem for the x86 architecture because of the vast popularity of Windows XP x86-32, many vendors choose to make 64-bit drivers only for Windows Vista—which means that Linux systems using the x86-64 architecture are unable to use such networking devices.

An archived version of the project's site and wiki is available [4].

See also

- OpenWrt
- Linux Unified Kernel

External links

- NDISwrapper website [1]
- The ndiswrapper wiki [5]
- NDISwrapper Installation [6] – An easy to follow video showing how to install NDISwrapper and get started with it.
- Ndisgtk [7]
- NdisConfig [8]
- Project Evil: The Evil Continues [9], 2004-01-24, Bill Paul on a FreeBSD mailing list
- Too Evil, Too Furious [10], 2005-04-25, Bill Paul on a FreeBSD mailing list
- NetBSD NDIS Driver Port [11]

References

[1] http://sourceforge.net/projects/ndiswrapper/
[2] http://www.linuxant.com/driverloader/
[3] "SourceForge.net: ndiswrapper" (http://ndiswrapper.sourceforge.net/joomla/index.php?/component/option,com_openwiki/Itemid,33/id,faq/). Ndiswrapper.sourceforge.net. 2009-07-12. . Retrieved 2009-09-21.
[4] http://web.archive.org/web/20080113194857/ndiswrapper.sourceforge.net/joomla/index.php?/component/option,com_openwiki/Itemid,33/id,list/
[5] http://sourceforge.net/apps/mediawiki/ndiswrapper/index.php?title=Main_Page
[6] http://linuxtutorialvideos.blogspot.com/2009/01/ndiswrapper.html
[7] http://jak-linux.org/projects/ndisgtk/
[8] http://code.google.com/p/ndisconfig/
[9] http://lists.freebsd.org/pipermail/freebsd-current/2004-January/019486.html
[10] http://lists.freebsd.org/pipermail/freebsd-hardware/2005-April/002464.html
[11] http://netbsd-soc.sourceforge.net/projects/ndis/

Nexus driver

The **term nexus** driver refers to a bus driver which interfaces leaf drivers to a specific I/O bus and provides the low-level integration of this I/O bus.

Omega Drivers

Type	Private Company
Founded	2004
Headquarters	, Puerto Rico
Key people	Angel Trinidad
Website	www.omegadrivers.net [1]

Omega Drivers are unofficial, third-party device drivers for ATi and NVIDIA graphics cards, created by Angel Trinidad. They differ from the official drivers in that they offer more customization and extra features. They are compatible with all ATi graphics cards and all NVIDIA cards that use Detonator drivers.

The drivers are tweaked versions of those officially released by ATi and NVIDIA, mainly using registry tweaks and offering an alternative installer. They are not custom drivers compiled from source code.

From the website:

> The purpose of the Omega Drivers is to provide gamers with an alternate set of drivers, ones that have more options and features than the original sets. The drivers contain optimizations, extra features (like OC capabilities), more resolutions and internal tweaks that can give them the edge in a gaming environment over the normal drivers, which are often tailored for synthetic benchmarks. All Omega driver sets are tested (unless noted) by myself in my own PC or in an alternate PC (in the case of the NVIDIA drivers) to ensure maximum compatibility and reliability.[2]

The drivers are even recognized by ATi as the best alternative drivers on the internet according to Terry Makedon:

> "ATi supports the enthusiast community wholly. Omega Drivers are in fact a good example of ATi's user community at its best. What they are in principle are CATALYST drivers with different settings enabled via registry keys and other such methods. This provides users an alternative to ATi's CATALYST default settings. While there are a few different modification drivers out in the community our relationship with the creator of the Omega Drivers is of the highest working standard. The author of these drivers is part of the CATALYST beta driver testing team, and also in direct contact with ATi. In fact we would go so far as to say that if a user chooses to go the mod driver route, they go with the Omega Drivers."[3]

NVIDIA has attempted legal action against some versions of Omega Drivers; later, Omega Drivers for NVIDIA cards were allowed to be made once again.[4]

ATi driver features

The Omega ATi driver is based on ATi's Catalyst drivers. The driver is particularly notable for resolving 3D compatibility problems affecting past versions of the ATi drivers (versions 7.8-7.12) and some AGP cards.

The driver includes various third party utilities including 'MultiRes' (from EnTech Taiwan) and ATI Tray Tools tweaking utility.

Current status

The Creator has just returned as of February 10th, 2010 with a slew of new drivers and updates.

ATi Tray Tool has not had a stable version since 2007.

External links

- Omega Drivers website [5]
- Omega Drivers support forum [6]

References

[1] http://www.omegadrivers.net/
[2] Omega drivers website - About section http://www.omegadrivers.net/about.php
[3] Interview with Ati's Terry Makedon by Nordic Hardware http://www.nordichardware.com/Articles/?skrivelse=335&page=1
[4] The case of Omega vs. NVIDIA http://translate.google.com/translate?hl=en&sl=de&u=http://www.wcm.at/story.php%3Fid%3D5316&sa=X&oi=translate&resnum=2&ct=result&prev=/search%3Fq%3D%2522There%2Bhas%2Bbeen%2Balot%2Bof%2Bdiscussion%2Brecently%2522%2Bnvidia%26hl%3Den%26lr%3D%26sa%3DG
[5] http://www.omegadrivers.net
[6] http://www.hardwareheaven.com

PC/TCP Packet Driver

PC/TCP Packet Driver is an API created in 1986 by FTP Software for network cards under x86-DOSes like FreeDOS, DR-DOS, MS-DOS, etc. It uses the x86 interrupt number (INT) between 0x60 .. 0x80. The exact number is detected at run-time. But it's usually 0x60.

An application scans through the handlers for vectors 0x60 through 0x80 until it finds one with the text string "PKT DRVR" in the 12 bytes immediately following the entry point.

The driver can handle Ethernet, Token ring, RS-232, Arcnet, X.25. [1]

Functions

Function name	AH number
driver_info	1
access_type	2
release_type	3
send_pkt	4
terminate	5
get_address	6
reset_interface	7
+get_parameters	10
+as_send_pkt	11
*set_rcv_mode	20
*get_rcv_mode	21
*set_multicast_list	22
*get_multicast_list	23
*get_statistics	24
*set_address	25

+ indicates a high-performance packet driver function

* indicates an extended packet driver function

See also

- Network Driver Interface Specification (NDIS)
- Open Data-Link Interface (ODI)
- Universal Network Device Interface (UNDI)

References

[1] "PC/TCP Packet Driver Specification" (http://www.crynwr.com/packet_driver.html). . 090430 crynwr.com

Printer driver

In computers, a **printer driver** or a **print processor** is a piece of software that converts the data to be printed to the form specific to a printer. The purpose of printer drivers is to allow applications to do printing without being aware of the technical details of each printer model.

Printer drivers should not be confused with print spoolers, that queue print jobs and send them to printer one after the other.

Printer drivers in different operating systems

Unix

On UNIX systems and other systems which use the Common Unix Printing System, such as Mac OS X, printer drivers are typically implemented as filters. They are usually named the *front end* of the printing system, while the printer spoolers constitute the *back end*.

Backends are also used to determinate the available devices. On startup, each backend is asked for a list of devices it supports, and any information that is available.

DOS

On MS-DOS, there have been no system-wide printer drivers; each application was shipped with its own printer drivers, which were essentially descriptions of printer commands. Printers, too, have been supplied with drivers for the most popular applications. In addition, applications included tools for editing printer description, in case there was no ready driver. In the days when DOS was widely used, many printers had emulation modes for Epson FX80[1] and IBM Proprinter commands. It appears that these also worked with Windows 3.0[2].

Windows

On Microsoft Windows systems, printer drivers make use of GDI (Unidrv or PScript-based) or XPS (XPSDrv). Programs then use the same standard APIs to draw text and pictures both on screen and on paper. Printers which use GDI natively are commonly referred to as Winprinters and are considered incompatible with other operating systems.

Win32 APIs also allow applications to send data directly to the spooler, bypassing the printer driver; however, few applications actually use this option.

Amiga

The original AmigaOS up to 1.3 supported printers through a standard series of drivers stored at the required path "DEVS:Printers". All printer drivers were stored in that directory, and covered the standard printers in 1985-1989 circa, included EpsonFX standard driver, XEROX 4020, HP, etcetera.

Any Amiga printer driver had to communicate though the standard Amiga printer.device (the default standard hardware device of Amiga dealing with printers), and the standard parallel.device (which controlled parallel port) and the driver would then control the printer on its own.

Amiga printers were an innovation for their time. The had the ability to print up to 4096 colors.

Through the use of the Printer Preferences program printers could be connected to the serial port as well.

Amiga also had support for a virtual device "PRT:" to refer to printer.device so, for example the command "COPY file TO PRT:" caused the file to be printed directly bypassing parallel.device and the default printer driver. Amiga used a standard ANSI "Esc sequences" list of ESC (Escape) Commands, not the special ones defined by the various printer manufacturers. This way every application on the Amiga could use the same standard set of control sequences and wouldn't need to know which printer is actually connected. The printer driver then translated these standard sequences into the special sequences a certain printer understands.

Amiga internal function "PWrite" of printer.device writes 'length' bytes directly to the printer. This function is generally called on by printer drivers to send their buffer(s) to the printer. Number of buffers are decided by the persons who created the driver. Amiga lacked a standard Printer Spooler.

Since AmigaOS 2.0 a standard printer.device was changed to control various printers at same time. The Printer preferences were divided in three main panels: *Prefs:Printer* which selects main printer and other basic elements such as "Print Spacing" and "Paper Size". *PrinterGFX* controlled features like Dithering and Scaling. *PrinterPS* controlled Postscript Printers. The printer drivers surprisingly remained almost same of Workbench 1.3, with 4096 limits.

This fact led Amiga users to prefer third party Printer Systems with their own drivers, like TurboPrint and PrintStudio, which introduced not only recent drivers, but also featured a functioning Printer Spooler into Amiga, and featured 16 millions colors printing. MorphOS Amiga clone Operating System uses a special version of TurboPrint to pilot recent printers.

Many Amiga programs like DTP programs as PageStream featured in the past its own printer drivers.

USB printers are automatically recognized by the Amiga USB Stack, which is called Poseidon. This stack is capable of detecting any USB device by its class, but printers still require a driver to be controlled.

PostScript printer description

Usually the operating system needs to know the characteristics of a printer. The PPD files are the normal way to supply this information. They have the advantage of being system independent, and there is a freely available large database of them, Foomatic.

See also

- PostScript Printer Description (PPD)
- CUPS
- Virtual printer
- XML Paper Specification (XPS)
- List of emulators
- ESC/P
- Printer Command Language (PCL)
- Windows Vista printing technologies

External links

- Amiga RKM [3] (ROM Kernel Manual), Printer. Device: provides detailed information about the Amiga's I/O subsystems.

Different brands and models in the printer driver download category. [4]

[1] for a list of Epson FX printer codes, see: (http://lprng.sourceforge.net/DISTRIB/RESOURCES/PPD/epson.htm)

[2] Citizen Printer Emulation Modes for Microsoft Windows 3.0 (http://support.microsoft.com/kb/69251)

[3] http://cataclysm.cx/random/amiga/reference/Devices_Manual_guide/node003E.html

[4] http://www.driverindirin.com/kategori/yazici-tarayici

SCSI Pass-Through Direct

Developer(s)	Duplex Secure, Ltd.
Stable release	1.69 / April 14, 2010
Operating system	Windows 2000 to Windows 7
License	Proprietary
Website	www.duplexsecure.com [1]

SCSI Pass Through Direct (usually abbreviated as **SPTD**, filename "sptd.sys") is a device driver developed by Duplex Secure Ltd. that provides a new method of access to storage devices. The SPTD API is not open to the public.

Implementations

SPTD is used by Daemon Tools and Alcohol 120%. It is also utilized in PowerArchiver Pro 2010 (v11.60+); however, a configurable option is available to disable it.[2] It is known to be incompatible with kernel-mode debugging including WinDbg and Microsoft's other command line debuggers as well as SoftICE. Further, certain versions of the freeware optical media burning software ImgBurn will issue a warning, "SPTD can have a detrimental effect on drive performance", if the application detects that SPTD is active/installed.

In the PowerArchiver Blog (see footnote above) of September 10, 2009, ConeXware (the maker of PowerArchiver) claims that in their internal testing SPTD improved optical drive burn rates by up to 20 percent versus "old school" SPTI.

See also

- Advanced SCSI Programming Interface (ASPI) from Adaptec is a publicly documented interface.
- SCSI Pass Through Interface (SPTI) from Microsoft is another publicly documented interface.
- ASAPI from Pinnacle Systems (see ASAPI download [2])
- Patin-Couffin

External links

- Duplex Secure home page [3]
- SCSI Port I/O Control Codes [4]

References

[1] http://www.duplexsecure.com/en/home
[2] http://www.powerarchiver.com/blog/2009/09/10/pa-2010-11-60-preview-3-improved-burner-experience/
[3] http://www.duplexsecure.com/
[4] http://msdn.microsoft.com/en-gb/library/ff565367.aspx

SIO (software)

SIO is a serial port driver package for OS/2 written by Raymond L. Gwinn. It is designed to not only improve performance over OS/2's default serial drivers, but also improve compatibility. SIO contains a virtualized FOSSIL (VX00) driver that can be loaded to provide FOSSIL support to DOS based communications software. SIO later added the ability to create virtualized COM ports, which, combined with the included program VMODEM, allows incoming telnet connections to be directed toward the virtualized COM port. Older communications software are also able to "call out" to telnet sites. This is possible due to a custom set of "AT" commands that allow users to pass a hostname to the VMODEM software. [1] .

SIO (and the included VMODEM software) became very popular among Bulletin Board System operators due to the incoming telnet feature, as well as drastic speed improvements over other telnet solutions of the time.

See also

- Ray Gwinn's story about the SIO-driver! [2]
- Download location of SIO/VMODEM [3]

References

[1] "THE OFFICIAL BBS FAQ: THE HISTORY OF FOSSIL DRIVERS" (http://www.sysopworld.com/bbsfaq/ch06.09.htm#6.09.02). . Retrieved 5 December 2008.

[2] http://www.os2world.com/content/view/14587/2/

[3] http://www.os2bbs.com/docs/access-details-vmodem.html

Scanner Access Now Easy

Stable release	1.0.21 / 25 April 2010
Operating system	Microsoft Windows, Linux, UNIX, OS/2
License	GNU General Public License (GPL)
Website	sane-project.org [1]

Scanner Access Now Easy (SANE) is an application programming interface (API) that provides standardized access to any raster image scanner hardware (flatbed scanner, handheld scanner, video- and still-cameras, frame grabbers, etc.).

The SANE API is public domain and its discussion and development is open to everybody. It is commonly used on Linux.

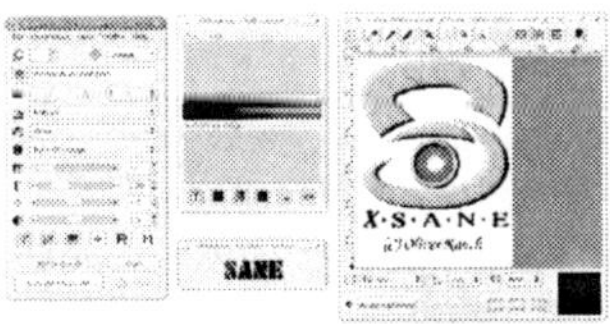

XSane on Ubuntu (Linux)

Development

SANE differs from TWAIN in that it is cleanly separated into frontends (user programs) and backends (scanner drivers). Whereas a TWAIN driver handles the user interface as well as communications with the scanner hardware, a SANE driver only provides an interface with the hardware and describes a number of "options" which drive each scan. These *options* specify parameters such as the resolution of the scan, the scan area, colour model, etc. Each *option* has a name, and information about its type, units, and range or possible values (e.g enumerated list). By convention there are several "well known" *options* that frontends can supply using convenient GUI interaction e.g. the scan area *options* can be set by dragging a rectangular outline over a preview image. Other options can be presented using GUI elements appropriate to their type e.g. sliders, drop-down lists, etc.

One consequence of this separation is that network scanning is easily implemented with no special handling in either the frontends or backends. On a host with a scanner, the **saned** daemon runs and handles network requests. On client machines a "net" backend (driver) connects to the remote host to fetch the scanner options, and perform previews and scans. The saned daemon acts as a frontend locally, but simply passes requests and data between the network connections and the local scanner. Similarly, the "net" backend passes requests and data between the local frontend and the remote host.

Various types of unsupervised batch scanning are also possible with a minimum of support needed in the backend (driver). Many scanners support the attachment of document feeders which allow a large number of sheets of paper to be automatically scanned in succession. Using the SANE API, the frontend simply has to "play back" the same set of options for each scan, driving the document feed in between scans to load the next sheet of paper. The frontend only has to obtain the set of options from the user once.

Graphical user interfaces

Several user interfaces have been written to combine SANE with an easy user method of controlling it.

XSane

XSane is a graphical frontend for SANE that is written and maintained by Oliver Rauch. It is available for Microsoft Windows, Linux, UNIX, and OS/2 and is licenced under the GNU General Public License (GPL)[2]

Simple Scan

Simple Scan is a simplified GUI using SANE that is intended to be easier to use and better integrate into the GNOME desktop than XSANE. It was initially written and is maintained by Robert Ancell of Canonical Ltd. for Linux. Simple Scan was first fielded as part of Ubuntu 10.04 Lucid Lynx.[3] [4] [5]

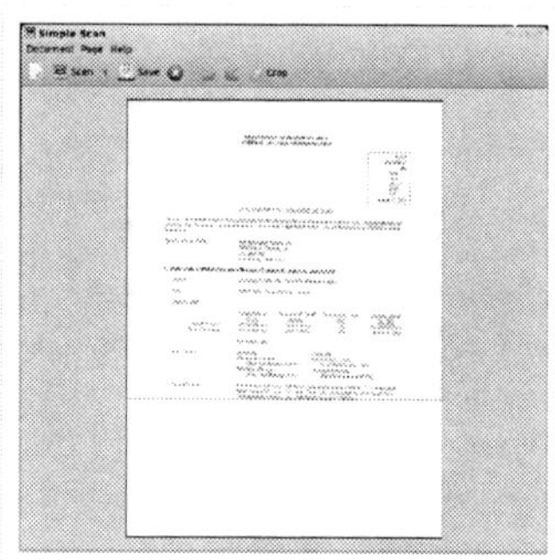

Simple Scan 1.0.3

See also

- Image and Scanner Interface Specification - Proprietary industry standard interface.
- TWAIN - Software API for local drivers that are bundled with control GUI.
- Windows Image Acquisition (WIA) - Proprietary API from Microsoft.

External links

- Official SANE website [1]
- Image Acquisition Framework for Java [6]
- SANE backends list [7]
- Java Tech: Acquire Images with TWAIN and SANE, Part 3 [8] by Jeff Friesen 04/11/2005

References

[1] http://www.sane-project.org/
[2] Rauch, Oliver (February 2009). "XSane - graphical scanning frontend" (http://www.xsane.org/). . Retrieved 4 June 2010.
[3] Ancell, Robert (May 2010). "Simple Scan" (https://launchpad.net/simple-scan). . Retrieved 4 June 2010.
[4] UbuntuUpdates.org (April 2010). "Package simple-scan" (http://www.ubuntuupdates.org/packages/show/167219). . Retrieved 4 June 2010.
[5] OMG! Ubuntu! (December 2009). "Lucid to Get Scanning Tool "Simple Scan"" (http://www.omgubuntu.co.uk/2009/12/lucid-to-get-new-scanning-tool-simple.html). . Retrieved 4 June 2010.
[6] http://www.gnome.sk/Twain/jtp.html
[7] http://www.sane-project.org/sane-backends.html
[8] http://today.java.net/pub/a/today/2005/04/11/twain.html

SciTech SNAP

SciTech SNAP (System Neutral Access Protocol) is an operating system portable, dynamically loadable, native-size 32-bit/64-bit device driver architecture. SciTech SNAP defines the architecture for loading an operating system neutral binary device driver for any type of hardware device, be it a graphics controller, audio controller, SCSI controller or network controller. SciTech SNAP drivers are source code portable between different microprocessor platforms, and the binary drivers are operating system portable within a particular microprocessor family.

SNAP drivers were originally developed for Intel 386+ CPU with any 32-bit operating system or environment supported on that CPU. With the introduction of SNAP 3.0, native binary SNAP drivers are available for 32-bit PowerPC CPUs and 64-bit x86-64 CPUs.

On 2002-8-27, SciTech Software, Inc. announced the intention to release the Scitech SNAP driver development kit.

On 2006-11-16, SciTech Software, Inc. announced that it has ceased further development of its SNAP device driver technology in favor of a new line of web and business logic technologies. SciTech also announced that it would begin looking for a buyer for SciTech SNAP.

In December 2008 Alt Richmond Inc.[1] closed the acquisition of SciTech Software's SNAP technology. The plans of SciTech Software in 2008 to create OpenSNAP, an open source version of the driver technology, are therefore no longer an option unless Alt Richmond decides to pick this up.

Relationship with Scitech Display Doctor

SciTech Display Doctor 6.5 included a replacement video driver for Windows 95 or higher, which works with any hardware supported by SDD. In SDD 7, the driver was renamed to Scitech Nucleus Graphics driver. The Nucleus Graphics driver was later incorporated into SciTech SNAP Graphics. In SNAP 3, Nucleus was renamed to SNAP.

SciTech SNAP Graphics version 2 also included VBETest/Lite - VESA BIOS Extensions (VBE) Compliance Test version 8.00. It was later removed in SciTech SNAP Graphics 3.

In SciTech SNAP 3 for DOS, most of the OpenGL tests from SciTech Display Doctor 7 beta can be found in GACtrl Driver Control Center.

Windows version of Scitech SNAP Graphics maintained the user interface found in SDD 7 beta.

SciTech SNAP Graphics

It is the first product for the SciTech SNAP line, which provides accelerated graphics.

SciTech SNAP Graphics has been ported to MS-DOS, OS/2, Microsoft Windows (CE, NT, 2000, XP), QNX, SMX (the SunOS/Solaris port of MINIX), Linux, On Time RTOS-32, Unununium OS operating systems. Supported hardware included video processors from 3dfx, 3Dlabs, Alliance Semiconductor, AMD (Geode GX2), ARK Logic, ATI, Chips & Technologies, Cirrus Logic, Cyrix, IBM, InteGraphics, Intel, Matrox, NeoMagic, Number Nine, NVIDIA, Oak, Philips, Rendition, S3, Sigma Designs, Silicon Motion, SiS, Tseng Labs, Trident, VIA, Weitek, as well as any video card supporting VBE 1.2 or higher.

Although SciTech SNAP Graphics does not offer standalone VBE driver, SNAP driver accelerates applications using VBE calls via SciTech SNAP Graphics driver. SNAP Graphics for Windows can also accelerate VBE 3 calls, if DOS programs is run in Windows DOS box.

Spin-off products

- SciTech SNAP Graphics ENT
- SciTech SNAP Graphics ENT/BC with DPVL support (SciTech SNAP Graphics VESA DPVL)
- SciTech SNAP Graphics IES

Personal Edition

SciTech also offer SciTech SNAP Graphics "PE" (Personal Edition) under the My SciTech site, which allows registered users to download a SNAP driver of hardware and operating system specified by users. Each user account can download 2 drivers per week. The driver generated by the service can be run for 6 months.

In Scitech SNAP Graphics PE, tools GACtrl, GAMode, GAOption, GAPerf DOS tools are included. The GLDirect tests are not included in Windows driver.

SciTech SNAP Audio

Similar to Scitech SNAP Graphics, it provides OS-independent audio drivers. It has been ported to Windows NT 4.0. Supported hardware include AC/97 and Intel HDA, but HDA does not support modem function.

SciTech SNAP DDC

It is designed to provide easy access to an attached display in order to program it directly via I^2C or simply to read the monitor's EDID record.

External links

- SciTech Software Inc. Announces that the Complete Source Code to its Leading Edge Graphics Driver Technology SciTech SNAP Graphics is for Sale [2]
- Alt Richmond Inc., the new owner of the SciTech SNAP technology [3]

References

[1] Alt Richmond Inc. closed the acquisition of SciTech Software's SNAP technology (http://www.altrichmond.ca/)
[2] http://www.scitechsoft.com/news/press/sale_of_snap.html
[3] http://www.altrichmond.ca/

SCSI Pass Through Interface

SCSI Pass Through Interface (SPTI) is a method for Microsoft Windows applications to access a SCSI I/O device.

Theory of Operation

The storage port drivers provide an interface for Win32 applications to send SCSI Command Descriptor Block (CDB) messages to SCSI devices. The interfaces are IOCTL_SCSI_PASS_THROUGH and IOCTL_SCSI_PASS_THROUGH_DIRECT. Applications can build a pass-through request and send it to the device by using this IOCTL.

API

The SPTI is accessible by Microsoft Windows application software by using the DeviceIoControl Windows API.[1]

Implementations

The ImgBurn application offers SPTI as a method for accessing optical disc drives.[2]

Other SCSI interfaces

- ASPI developed by Adaptec, Nero AG, Pinnacle Systems
- ASAPI.DLL SCSI Pass Through Interface (ASAPI) developed by VOB Computersysteme GmbH, owned by Pinnacle Systems
- Elby CDIO developed by Elaborate Bytes
- SCSI Pass-Through Direct (SPTD) developed by Duplex Secure Ltd

See also

- Windows Driver Kit

External link

- SCSI Pass Through Interface [3]

References

[1] "Windows Driver Kit: Storage Devices: SCSI Pass Through Interface" (http://msdn.microsoft.com/en-us/library/dd163410.aspx). . Retrieved 8 August 2009.
[2] "ImgBurn Support Forum" (http://forum.imgburn.com/lofiversion/index.php/t6659.html). . Retrieved 8 August 2009.
[3] http://msdn.microsoft.com/en-us/library/dd163410.aspx

Uniform Driver Interface

The **Uniform Driver Interface** (**UDI**) is a defunct project developed by several companies to define a portable interface for device drivers.

The Uniform Driver Interface (UDI) allowed device drivers to be portable across both hardware platforms and operating systems without any changes to the driver source. With the participation of multiple OS, platform and device hardware vendors, UDI was intended to be the first interface which was likely to achieve such portability on a wide scale. UDI provided an encapsulating environment for drivers with well-defined interfaces which isolated drivers from OS policies and from platform and I/O bus dependencies. In principle, this allowed driver development to be totally independent of OS development. In addition, the UDI architecture was intended to insulate drivers from platform specifics such as byte-ordering, DMA implications, multi-processing, interrupt implementations and I/O bus topologies.

While UDI could potentially benefit open source operating systems such as Linux and *BSD by providing more driver support from companies, some open source/free software advocates feared that UDI would cause a proliferation of closed source drivers and a reduction in open source support by companies, undermining the purpose of the free software and open source movements. Richard Stallman (the leader of the free software movement) has claimed that the project does not benefit the free software movement. [1]

See also

- I2O
- Network Driver Interface Specification (NDIS)
- Open Data-Link Interface (ODI)
- Universal Network Device Interface (UNDI)
- PC/TCP Packet Driver

References

1. Richard Stallman (1998). "UDI and Free Software" [1]. Linux Today. Retrieved 2007-06-18.
2. Software Technologies Group (2001-05-09). "UDI Reference Implementation Open Sourced" [2]. Press release.

External links

- Project UDI [3]
- UDI Reference Implementation [4]

References

[1] http://linuxtoday.com/developer/1998100500205OP
[2] http://www.stg.com/press_releases/050901.html
[3] http://www.projectudi.org/
[4] http://projectudi.sourceforge.net/

UniVBE

UniVBE (short for **Universal VESA BIOS Extensions**) is a software driver that allows DOS applications written to the VESA BIOS standard to run on almost any display device made in the last 15 years or so.

The UniVBE driver was written by SciTech Software and is also available in their product called **SciTech Display Doctor**.

The primary benefit is increased compatibility and performance with DOS games. Many video cards have sub-par implementations of the VESA standards, or no support at all. UNIVBE replaces the card's built-in support. Many DOS games include a version of UNIVBE because VESA issues were so widespread.

According to SciTech Software Inc, SciTech Display Doctor is licensed by IBM as the native graphics driver solution for OS/2.[1]

History

The software started out as The Universal VESA TSR (UNIVESA), written by Kendall Bennett. It was renamed to Universal VESA BIOS Extensions (UniVBE) in version 5, which supports VBE/Core 2.0, and no longer a freeware.

In version 5.2, it was renamed to Scitech Display Doctor. However, UniVBE continued to be the name used for the actual driver.

Version 6 included support of VBE/Core 3.0, VBE/SCI.

Version 6.5 introduced the ability to use Scitech Display Doctor as wrapper video driver.

Version 7 supports VESA/MCCS, and included Scitech GLDirect, an OpenGL emulator. This version was also ported to OS/2 and Linux (as version 1.0). However, the proposed product has never been widely available. Only pre-releases are available to public. In the Windows SDD prerelease, it included DOS UniVBE driver 7.20 beta, the Scitech Nucleus Graphics driver, GLDirect 2.0 and 3.0 beta. SDD 7 was first released on OS/2 on 2002-02-28, followed by Windows beta on 2002-03-01.

SciTech Display Doctor 7.1 marked the final release of SDD, which was available on OS/2, among other operating systems. However, the Scitech Nucleus Graphics engine lived on as SciTech SNAP (System Neutral Access Protocol) Graphics, SciTech SNAP DDC, and SciTech VBE Test Suite 8.0.[2] Unlike UniVBE, SciTech SNAP Graphics is designed as fully accelerated binary compatible graphic device driver, rather than patching a GPU BIOS to be VESA-compliant.

Display Doctor is no longer supported by SciTech Software. SciTech Display Doctor 5.3a, SciTech Display Doctor 6.53, and UniVBE 6.7 were available on their FTP site [3], but as of 2009-10-04, the FTP site no longer seems to be available; this seems to be related to the acquisition of SciTech Software by Alt Richmond Inc. 2008-12. Please see the SciTech SNAP article for more details.

One attempt to provide an alternative to SciTech's products was FreeBE/AF [4], but the last release was 1998-06-27, and the project author describes it as "dead" on his home page.

Compatibility

UniVBE requires a video card with at least 512 KB of memory.

Although UniVBE has supported many controllers, the quality of VESA support decayed in newer incarnations, especially for owners with older hardware. In the case of newer GPUs, the video cards that use them have begun to incorporate rewritable firmware, which allows video card manufacturers to offer better VBE patches than SciTech can supply, especially for cards using Matrox processors.

UniVBE does not add 16-colour screen modes or text modes, but offers an option to reuse those modes with a "pass through feature." However, the text mode pass through feature has been broken since the release of SDD 6.

Matrox G-series video cards can only use video modes that utilize at most half of its memory. This is different from the Matrox Millennium, which was documented by SciTech as a hardware flaw.

External links

- Definition from the Encyclopedia of Computing Terms [5]
- SciTech Software Inc. [6]

References

[1] http://www.scitechsoft.com/about/about.html
[2] http://www.scoug.com/OS24U/2002/scoug209.download.html
[3] http://www.scitechsoft.com/ftp/sdd/
[4] http://www.talula.demon.co.uk/freebe/
[5] http://www.pcmag.com/encyclopedia_term/0,2542,t=UniVBE&i=53447,00.asp
[6] http://www.scitechsoft.com

Universal Audio Architecture

Universal Audio Architecture (UAA) is an initiative unveiled in 2002 by Microsoft to standardize the hardware and class driver architecture for audio devices in modern Microsoft Windows operating systems. Three classes of audio devices are supported by default: USB, IEEE 1394 (Firewire), and Intel High Definition Audio, which supports PCI and PCI Express.

Starting with Windows Vista, Microsoft requires all computer and audio device manufacturers to support Universal Audio Architecture in order to pass Windows Logo.

Overview

The goal of the Universal Audio Architecture is to solve a very common problem in modern Microsoft Windows products, that of inconsistent support for audio. Due to the lack of a common system by which audio devices could describe their capabilities to the operating system, not to mention a lack of ability to control those capabilities, audio device manufacturers (such as Creative Labs, Realtek, Turtle Beach and others) have had to provide a series of control panels and custom interfaces to let a user control the device. This, in turn, requires kernel-mode drivers so that the user's actions can be communicated to the hardware itself. Poorly-written audio drivers have been a common source of system instability in Windows, especially with games that make use of extended audio card capabilities. These concerns prompted Microsoft to disable the audio stack entirely by default in Windows Server 2003.

UAA seeks to resolve problems by putting forth a standardized interface which audio devices can follow, ensuring that the device's capabilities will be recognized and used effectively by Windows, without the need for additional drivers or custom control panels. It also provides a reasonable assurance that an audio device will still be able to work many years down the road, without requiring vendor-supplied drivers for a newer version of Windows.

Another goal of UAA is to provide better support for multi-channel audio in Windows so that, for example, multi-channel WMA Pro audio streams can be played without special driver support.

UAA is intended to be a complete replacement for developing WDM Audio Drivers; however, in some cases it may be necessary for an otherwise UAA-compliant audio device to expose capabilities that cannot be done through UAA. Windows will continue to fully support audio drivers that use the PortCls and AVStream drivers.[1]

History

In 2004, Microsoft provided the first version of UAA as an update to Windows 2000 Service Pack 4, Windows XP Service Pack 1 and Windows Server 2003, but is only available by contacting Microsoft support directly.[2] However, almost all manufacturer supplied drivers contain the UAA class driver. Windows XP Service Pack 3 also includes the updated driver.

In Windows Vista, the Windows Logo program requirements state that any machine shipped with Vista must include a UAA-compliant audio device that works without additional drivers.

External links

- Audio Device Technologies for Windows [3] — Windows Hardware Developer Center web site
- Universal Audio Architecture (UAA) High Definition Audio class driver (Q888111) for Windows XP with Service Pack 1 [4]

See also

- Windows Vista audio architecture
- Windows legacy audio components

References

[1] Getting Started with WDM Audio Drivers (http://www.microsoft.com/whdc/device/audio/wdmaud-drv.mspx) provides further information on when it is appropriate to develop a custom audio driver.

[2] MSKB 835221 (http://support.microsoft.com/kb/835221/) describes the initial driver release, and MKSB 888111 (http://support.microsoft.com/kb/888111/) describes the 1.0a update.

[3] http://www.microsoft.com/whdc/device/audio/default.mspx

[4] http://www-307.ibm.com/pc/support/site.wss/document.do?sitestyle=lenovo&lndocid=MIGR-65440

User space

A conventional computer operating system usually segregates virtual memory into **kernel space** and **user space**. Kernel space is strictly reserved for running the kernel, kernel extensions, and most device drivers. In contrast, user space is the memory area where all user mode applications work and this memory can be swapped out when necessary.

Similarly, the term **userland** refers to all application software that runs in user space.[1] Userland usually refers to the various programs and libraries that the operating system uses to interact with the kernel: software that performs input/output, manipulates file system objects, etc.

Each user space process normally runs in its own virtual memory space, and, unless explicitly requested, cannot access the memory of other processes. This is the basis for memory protection in today's mainstream operating systems, and a building block for privilege separation. Depending on the privileges, processes can request the kernel to map part of another process' memory space to its own, as is the case for debuggers. Programs can also request shared memory regions with other processes.

Another approach taken in experimental operating systems is to have a single address space for all software, and rely on the programming language's virtual machine to make sure that arbitrary memory cannot be accessed — applications simply cannot acquire any references to the objects that they are not allowed to access.[2] This approach has been implemented in JXOS, Unununium as well as Microsoft's Singularity research project.

See also

- Memory protection
- Ring (computer security)
- CPU modes

References

[1] "userland, n." (http://www.catb.org/jargon/html/U/userland.html). *The Jargon File*. Eric S. Raymond. . Retrieved 2010-04-30.

[2] What kind of kernel does Unununium have? (http://unununium.org/)

User-Mode Driver Framework

The **User-Mode Driver Framework** is a device-driver development platform first introduced with Microsoft's Windows Vista operating system, and is also available for Windows XP. It facilitates the creation of drivers for certain classes of devices.

Overview

Badly written drivers can cause severe damage to a system since all drivers have high privileges when accessing the kernel directly. The User-Mode Driver Framework is not able to access the kernel directly but instead accesses it through a dedicated application programming interface. If an error occurs, the new framework allows for an immediate restart of the driver without impacting the system. Typically, devices are connected to the computer through a bus technology such as USB or Firewire.

The first version of the UMDF was shipped as part of Windows Media Player version 10. Code-named "Crescent", it was designed to support the Media Transfer Protocol driver, and no public interfaces or documentation were provided for it. Later, Microsoft decided to turn UMDF into a device driver development platform.[1]

The current version of the User-Mode Driver Framework is 1.7, which shipped as part of Windows Vista Service Pack 1 and Windows Server 2008, and is available for Windows XP Service Pack 2 and later, and Windows Server 2003 Service Pack 2 and later.[2]

Architecture

A UMDF Driver is a DLL based on Microsoft's Component Object Model (COM). However, UMDF does not use COM for loading, unloading, or controlling concurrency; it only uses COM only as a programming pattern, for example exploiting COM's *IUnknown* interface. At startup, UMDF calls *DllGetClassObject* to get a pointer to an *IClassFactory* interface in the driver and then uses the *CreateInstance* method of the IClassFactory interface to create an instance of the driver object.

The driver object is an instance of the framework-provided *IWDFDriver* interface. The driver provides a set of callbacks via the *IDriverEntry* COM interface, which is the main entry point for driver customization.

See also

- Windows Driver Foundation
- Kernel-Mode Driver Framework

External links

- User-Mode Driver Framework Homepage [3]
- Peter Wieland's blog [4] – developer lead on the UMDF team at Microsoft

References

[1] Charles Torre, Peter Wieland (2006-09-18). "Peter Wieland: User Mode Driver Framework" (http://channel9.msdn.com/showpost.aspx?postid=236023). *Channel 9*. Microsoft. . Retrieved 2006-09-18.

[2] Tsigkogiannis, Ilias (December 13, 2007). "WDF 1.7 RC1 has been released!" (http://blogs.msdn.com/iliast/archive/2007/12/13/wdf-1-7-rc1-has-been-released.aspx). *Ilias Tsigkogiannis' Introduction to Windows Device Drivers*. MSDN Blogs. . Retrieved 2008-07-22.

[3] http://www.microsoft.com/whdc/driver/wdf/UMDF.mspx

[4] http://blogs.msdn.com/peterwie/

Vidix

Developer(s)	Nickols_K
Stable release	1.0.0 / April 7, 2007
Operating system	Linux
Type	Device driver
License	GPL
Website	vidix.sourceforge.net [1]

VIDIX (*video interface for *nix*) is a portable interface which was designed and introduced as an interface to userspace drivers to provide DGA (Direct Graphics Access).

History

The idea to create **Vidix** was born as an alternative to the poorly designed linux-kernel based drivers from the mplayerhq project. For a long time **vidix** lived within the mplayerhq project then later it lived within the mplayerxp project. At that early time it was not seen as an independent project. During that time linux and many other unix clones lacked quality drivers for the video subsystems. Almost all video-related documentation was under NDA at the time and many hackers had to code their drivers blindly. With the help of many other volunteers the **vidix** project was born. Other developers became interested in using it for their own players and they asked the author of **vidix** to separate it from the mplayerxp project. Later **Vidix** became an alternative set of drivers which were based on the idea of direct hardware access similar to Windows' DirectX. These drivers just mapped accelerated video memory to avoid colour-space conversion and software scaling from the side of the players. Today **vidix** is being used by many other video players because it became a standalone project perfectly separated from mplayerhq and mplayerxp. The author of mplayerxp (fork of mplayerhq) still continues development of **vidix** regardless of the existence of the newest dri2 extension of the X system and the ability of commercially available drivers from the side of hardware vendors.

Philosophy

In short, the philosophy of **vidix** may be pointed as: *"to be traditionally available package of video drivers for *nix players"*. It's just a free package of drivers which are tuned for video playback projects. They covers almost all needs of video-players and provide simplest abstraction layer for them.

Supported hardware

- Cyberblade/i1
- Hauppage PVR350
- ATI Mach64 and 3dRage chips
- Matrox MGA chips
- some NVidia chips
- 3DLabs Permedia 2(3) and GLINT R3
- almost all ATI Radeons and Rage128 chips
- S3 Savage series
- SIS 300, 310 and 325 chips

- VIA Cle266 Unichrome

See also

- Driver
- Video
- Framebuffer
- Video card

External links

- Home page of VIDIX [1]
- Mplayerxp

References

[1] http://vidix.sourceforge.net

VxD

VxD is the device driver model used in Microsoft Windows/386, the 386 enhanced mode of Windows 3.x, and Windows 9x. VxDs have access to the memory of the kernel and all running processes, as well as raw access to the hardware.

Design

The name "VxD" is an abbreviation for "virtual xxx driver", where "xxx" is some class of hardware device. It derives from the fact that most drivers had filenames of the form vxxxd.386 in Windows 3.x. Some examples are: vjoyd.386 (joystick), vmm.386 (memory manager). VxDs usually have the filename extension .386 under Windows 3.x and .vxd under Windows 95. VxDs written for Windows 3.x can be used under Windows 95 but not vice versa.

History

Prior to the advent of Windows, DOS applications would either communicate directly with the various pieces of hardware (responding to interrupts, reading and writing device memory etc.) or go through a DOS Device Driver. As DOS was not multitasking each application would have exclusive and complete control over the hardware while running. Though Windows applications don't often communicate directly with hardware, it was the only way to write Windows drivers, and still is in the real and standard modes of Windows 3.x. Despite the fact that Windows switched from running in real mode to protected mode, direct hardware access and interrupt hooking could still be done because when Windows switched to running in protected mode it kept the single privilege level model used in real mode. This lasted all the way through Windows 9x. Windows/386 and onwards allowed multiple MS-DOS applications to execute simultaneously. This was done by executing each legacy application within its own virtual machine. To share arbitrary physical resources amongst these virtual machines, Microsoft introduced dynamically-loadable virtual device drivers. These drivers solved issues relating to conflicting usage of physical resources by intercepting calls to the hardware. Instead of a machine port representing an actual device, it would represent a "virtual" device, which could be managed by the operating system.

Obsolescence

Although Windows 98 introduced the Windows Driver Model, VxD device drivers can be used under Windows 98 and Windows Me. VxDs are not usable in Windows NT or its descendants. Starting with Windows 2000, Windows NT-based operating systems also use the Windows Driver Model (WDM), while Windows NT 4 and earlier versions must use drivers written specifically for them. Using VxD drivers instead of WDM drivers in Windows 9x resulted in advanced ACPI states like Hibernation (computing) being unavailable.

VxDs should not to be confused with the similar NTVDM-specific 'Virtual Device Drivers', which provide a method of emulating direct I/O under a Windows NT "DOS Box". NTVDM VDDs run as regular, 32-bit, user-mode DLL's, and must rely on the Win32 API (or another WDM driver) to emulate the desired I/O on behalf of the 16-bit program.

Windows Display Driver Model

Windows Display Driver Model (**WDDM**, also **WVDDM** during the Vista time-frame) is the graphic driver architecture for video card drivers running Microsoft Windows versions beginning with Windows Vista.[1]

It is a replacement for the Windows XP display driver architecture aimed at enabling better performance graphics and new graphics functionality.[1]

WDDM provides the functionality required to render the desktop and applications using Desktop Window Manager, a compositing window manager running on top of Direct3D. It also supports new DXGI interfaces required for basic device management and creation. The WDDM specification requires at least Direct3D 9-capable video card and the display driver must implement the device driver interfaces for the Direct3D 9Ex runtime in order to run legacy Direct3D applications; it may optionally implement runtime interfaces for Direct3D 10/10.1 and higher.

Features enabled by the WDDM

WDDM drivers enable new areas of functionality which were not uniformly provided by earlier display driver models. These include:

Virtualized video memory

In the context of graphics, virtualization means that individual processes (in userland) cannot see the memory of adjacent processes even by means of insertion of forged commands in the command stream. WDDM drivers allow video memory to be virtualized [2] , and video data to be paged out of video memory into system RAM. In case the video memory available turns out to be insufficient to store all the video data and textures, currently unused data is moved out to system RAM or to the disk. When the swapped out data is needed, it is fetched back. Virtualization could be supported on previous driver models (such as the XP Driver Model) to some extent, but was the responsibility of the driver, instead of being handled at the runtime level.

Scheduling

The runtime handles scheduling of concurrent graphics contexts.[3] Each list of commands is put in a queue for execution by the GPU, and it can be preempted by the runtime if a more critical task arrives and if it has not begun execution. This differs from native threads on the CPU where one task cannot be interrupted and therefore can take longer than necessary and make the computer appear less responsive. A hybrid scheduling algorithm between native and light threads with cooperation between the threads would achieve seamless parallelism. It is important to note that scheduling is not a new concept but it was previously the responsibility of individual driver developers. WDDM attempts to unify the experience across different vendors by controlling the execution of GPU tasks.

Cross-process sharing of Direct3D surfaces

A Direct3D graphics surface is the memory area that contains information about the textured meshes used for rendering a 2D or 3D scene. WDDM allows Direct3D surfaces to be shared across processes [4] . Thus, an application can incorporate a mesh created by another application into the scene it is rendering. Sharing textures between processes before WDDM was difficult, as it would have required copying the data from video memory to system memory and then back to video memory for the new device.

Enhanced fault-tolerance

If a WDDM driver hangs or encounters a fault, the graphics stack will restart the driver.[1] A graphics hardware fault will be intercepted and if necessary the driver will be reset.

Drivers under Windows XP were free to deal with hardware faults as they saw fit either by reporting it to the user or by attempting to recover silently. With a WDDM driver, all hardware faults cause the driver to be reset and the user will be notified by a popup; this unifies the behavior across vendors.

Previous drivers were fully implemented in kernel mode, whereas WDDM is implemented partly in user mode. If the user mode area fails with an unrecoverable error, it will, at the most, cause the application to quit unexpectedly instead of producing a blue screen error as it would in previous driver models.

WDDM also allows the graphic hardware to be reset or unplugged without a proper reboot. In practice, a driver update should not necessitate a reboot.

Need for a new display driver model

One of the chief scenarios the Windows Display Driver Model enables is the Desktop Window Manager. Since the desktop and application windows managed by DWM are Direct3D applications, the number of open windows directly affects the amount of video memory required. Because there is no limit on the number of open windows, the video memory available may prove insufficient, necessitating virtualization. As the window contents that DWM composes into the final desktop are generated by different processes, cross-process surface sharing is necessary. Also, because there can be other DirectX applications running alongside DWM on the DWM-managed desktop, they must be able to access the GPU in a shared manner, necessitating scheduling.

Though this is true for Microsoft's implementation of a composited desktop under Windows Vista, on the other hand, a composited desktop need not theoretically require a new display driver model to work as expected. Successful implementations of composited desktops were done before Windows Vista on other platforms such as Quartz, Compiz, WindowFX. The approach Microsoft attempted was to try to make sure WDDM was a unified experience across different GPUs from multiple vendors by standardizing their features and performance. The software features missing from other driver models could be made immaterial by extensions or if a less restrictive or simply different driver model was in place.

Limitations

The new driver model requires the graphics hardware to have Shader Model 2.0 support at least (fixed function pipeline is now translated to 2.0 shaders). However, according to Microsoft, as of 2009, only about 1-2 percent of hardware used the XPDM[5] , with the rest already WDDM capable. It also requires some other hardware features (causing, for example, SM 2.0-supporting hardware such as Intel GMA 900 to fail the WDDM certification [6]).

One of the limitations of WDDM driver model version **1.0** is that it does not support multiple drivers in a multi-adapter, multi-monitor setup. If a multi-monitor system has more than one graphics adapter powering the monitors, both the adaptors must use the same WDDM driver. If more than one driver is used, Windows will disable one of them.[7] . WDDM 1.1 does not have this limitation.[8]

WDDM 1.0/1.1 does not allow some modes that were previously handled by the driver such as spanning mode (stretching the desktop across two monitors) [9] [10] although *Dual View* [11] is still available.[12]

WDDM 1.1

Windows 7 supports major additions to WDDM tentatively known as WDDM 1.1; the details of this new version were unveiled at WinHEC 2008. New features include [5] :

- DXGI 1.1, which features return of 2D GUI hardware acceleration for use by GDI [13] and Direct2D/DirectWrite (but not GDI+)
  - BitBlt, StretchBlt, TransparentBlt
  - AlphaBlend, ColorFill
  - ClearType font support
- Direct3D 11 Device Driver Interface (DDI)
- DXVA-HD DDI [14]
- Hardware video overlay DDI [15]
- Optional AES 128 encryption
- Optional decoding of encrypted video content
- Support multiple drivers in a multi-adapter and multi-monitor setup [5] [16]

Hardware acceleration of GDI and Direct2D/DirectWrite operations helps reduce memory footprint in Windows 7, because DWM compositing engine no longer needs to keep a system memory copy of all surfaces used by GDI/GDI+, as in Windows Vista.[17] [18]

WDDM 1.1, Direct3D 11, Direct2D and DirectWrite will also be available with Windows Vista Platform Update; however GDI/GDI+ in Vista will continue to rely on software rendering [19] and the Desktop Window Manager will continue to use Direct3D 9Ex.[20]

WDDM 1.1 drivers are backward compatible with WDDM 1.0 specification; both 1.0 and 1.1 drivers can be used in Windows Vista with or without the Platform Update.[5]

Future versions

WDDM 2.0

At WinHEC 2006, Microsoft talked about how it was planning a major change to WDDM to allow for better multitasking on GPUs. According to Microsoft, WDDM 1.0 only allows rudimentary task scheduling with rendering "batch queue" granularity. **WDDM 2.0** and **WDDM 2.1**, which at that time were expected post-Vista[21] but on which Microsoft had not put an introduction date, would offer fine grain preemptive multitasking and would require a new generation of GPUs.[22] [23]

External links

- MSDN - WDDM Introduction [24]
- List of GPUs supporting WDDM [25]

References

[1] Windows Vista Display Driver Model (http://msdn.microsoft.com/en-us/library/aa480220.aspx)

[2] Graphics Memory Reporting in WDDM (http://download.microsoft.com/download/9/c/5/9c5b2167-8017-4bae-9fde-d599bac8184a/GraphicsMemory.doc)

[3] The role of the Windows Display Driver Model in the DWM (http://blogs.msdn.com/greg_schechter/archive/2006/04/02/566767.aspx)

[4] Cross Process Resource Sharing (http://msdn.microsoft.com/en-us/library/dd327290.aspx)

[5] "WHDC: Graphics Guide for Windows 7" (http://www.microsoft.com/whdc/device/display/GraphicsGuideWin7.mspx). Microsoft. 12-06-2009. .

[6] Intel excuse for no GMA900 WDDM driver: no "HW Scheduler" no driver (http://forum.beyond3d.com/showthread.php?t=35048), Beyond3D, October 26, 2006.

[7] "MultiMonitor Support and Windows Vista" (http://www.microsoft.com/whdc/device/display/multimonVista.mspx). . Retrieved 2007-10-20.

[8] Working With the Windows 7 Graphics Architecture: WinHEC 2008 (http://download.microsoft.com/download/5/E/6/5E66B27B-988B-4F50-AF3A-C2FF1E62180F/GRA-T584_WH08.pptx)

[9] Are there Control Panel features that were available under Windows XP that are no longer available on Windows Vista? (http://nvidia.custhelp.com/cgi-bin/nvidia.cfg/php/enduser/std_adp.php?p_faqid=2026)

[10] Stretched Desktop or Spanning Mode Not Available in Catalyst Control Center Under Windows Vista (http://support.amd.com/us/kbarticles/Pages/26771-stretched-mode-Catalyst-Control-Center.aspx)

[11] Description of DualView in Windows XP (http://support.microsoft.com/kb/283674)

[12] MultiMonitor Support and Windows Vista (http://www.microsoft.com/whdc/device/display/multimonVista.mspx)

[13] "Windows DDK - GDI Hardware Acceleration" (http://msdn.microsoft.com/en-us/library/ff566559.aspx). MSDN. . Retrieved 2009-06-14.

[14] "Windows DDK - DXVA-HD DDI" (http://msdn.microsoft.com/en-us/library/ff568661.aspx). MSDN. . Retrieved 2009-06-13.

[15] "Windows DDK - Overlay DDI" (http://msdn.microsoft.com/en-us/library/ff563972.aspx). MSDN. . Retrieved 2009-06-13.

[16] "Windows DDK - Multiple Monitors and Video Present Networks" (http://msdn.microsoft.com/en-us/library/ff568500(v=VS.85).aspx). MSDN. . Retrieved 2010-07-14.

[17] Greg Schechter's Blog: Redirecting GDI, DirectX, and WPF applications (http://blogs.msdn.com/greg_schechter/archive/2006/05/02/588934.aspx)

[18] Engineering Windows 7 Graphics Performance (http://blogs.msdn.com/e7/archive/2009/04/25/engineering-windows-7-for-graphics-performance.aspx)

[19] Introducing the Microsoft Direct2D API (http://blogs.technet.com/thomasolsen/archive/2008/10/29/introducing-the-microsoft-direct2d-api.aspx)

[20] Mark Lawrence (2009-11-25). "Internet Explorer announces to use DirectWrite & Direct2D (comment from Microsoft official)" (http://blogs.msdn.com/directx/archive/2009/11/18/internet-explorer-announces-to-use-directwrite-direct2d.aspx). .

[21] WinHEC 2006: Display Driver Logistics And Testing (http://download.microsoft.com/download/5/b/9/5b97017b-e28a-4bae-ba48-174cf47d23cd/PRI023_WH06.ppt)

[22] WinHEC 2006: Windows Display Driver Model (WDDM) v2 And Beyond (http://download.microsoft.com/download/5/b/9/5b97017b-e28a-4bae-ba48-174cf47d23cd/PRI103_WH06.ppt)

[23] Dan Warne (June 1, 2006). "Windows graphics system to be overhauled" (http://www.apcstart.com/site/dwarne/2006/06/193/windows-graphics-system-to-be-overhauled). APC Magazine. . Retrieved 2006-06-02.

[24] http://msdn2.microsoft.com/en-us/library/aa480220

[25] http://technet.microsoft.com/en-us/windows/aa905088.aspx

Windows Driver Foundation

Developer(s)	Microsoft
Stable release	1.9
Development status	Active
Operating system	Windows
Available in	English

Windows Driver Foundation (WDF) is a set of Microsoft tools that aid in the creation of device drivers for Windows 2000 and later versions of Windows.

The primary tools that comprise WDF are the Kernel Mode Driver Framework (KMDF) and User Mode Driver Framework (UMDF). These tool kits provide a new, object-oriented, programming model for Windows driver development. The primary goal of the Frameworks is "Conceptual Scalability", that is the characteristics of only requiring a driver developer to learn a few simple concepts to be able to write a simple driver, and to be able to incrementally learn more when more complex driver features are required. This differs markedly from the Windows Driver Model (WDM) that requires driver developers to be fully familiar with many complex technical details before writing even a simple driver.

Part of the key to achieving Conceptual Scalability is that KMDF and UMDF use an "opt-in" model. This model allows the developer to extend and override the default behavior of a canonical "good driver". This is in contrast to the older Windows Driver Model that depends on the driver writer to implement all aspects of the driver's behavior.

Varieties

The Framework comes in two varieties:

- The Kernel-Mode Driver Framework, for writing standard kernel-mode device drivers.
- The User-Mode Driver Framework, for writing certain classes of driver that can run in user-mode.

These share the underlying programming model. However, the kernel-mode framework uses a flat C API while the user-mode framework is based on C++ and a light version of COM.

WDF also includes a set of static verification tools for use by driver writers. These tools examine driver code for common errors and/or simulate the code of a driver in order to identify problems that are both difficult to detect and difficult to test for.

Tools

The Static Driver Verifier (SDV) is capable of performing very deep validation of code paths across functions and even through calls into WDM. SDV can find driver problems that span multiple function calls and even multiple operations. SDV is designed to be run when the driver is nearing completion. SDV analyzes only C files, C++ is not supported.

PREFast for Drivers (PFD) performs rather shallow analysis of driver operations. PFD can check for buffer overruns and other common programming errors likewise a number of driver specific problems. Because its scope of operation is within a single function, PFD's run time is much shorter than SDV. Therefore, PFD can be used throughout the driver development process. PREFast scans each function as isolated unit, it does not do inter-procedural analysis. [1]

External links

- Windows Driver Foundation Homepage [2]
- *Developing Drivers with the Windows Driver Foundation* [3] by Orwick and Smith
- Windows Driver Kit [2]
- [4] OSR Online, including many articles about WDF, KMDF, and Windows driver development.
- Introducing Windows Driver Framework [1], written by well-known Windows driver developer, Walter Oney.
- Building and deploying a basic WDF Kernel Mode Driver [5], CodeProject
- Developing a WDF USB Kernel Mode Driver for the OSR USB FX2 [6], CodeProject

References

[1] http://msdn.microsoft.com/en-us/library/ff546187.aspx
[2] http://www.microsoft.com/whdc/driver/wdf/default.mspx
[3] http://www.microsoft.com/whdc/driver/wdf/wdfbook.mspx
[4] http://www.osronline.com
[5] http://www.codeproject.com/system/wdf_kmdf_basic.asp
[6] http://www.codeproject.com/system/kmdf_osr_usb_fx2.asp

Windows Driver Kit

Developer(s)	Microsoft
Stable release	7.1.0
Preview release	7.1.0
Development status	Active
Operating system	Windows
Available in	English
Website	Windows Driver Kit [1]

The **Windows Driver Kit** (WDK) is a software toolset from Microsoft that enables the development of device drivers for the Microsoft Windows platform. It includes documentation, samples, build environments, and tools for driver developers.

History of WDK

Previously, the WDK was known as Windows Driver Development Kit (DDK) and supported Windows Driver Model development. It got its current name when Microsoft released Windows Vista and added the following tools to the kit:

- Windows Driver Foundation (WDF)
- Installable File System Kit (IFS Kit)
- Driver Test Manager (DTM)

Later DTM was renamed to Windows Logo Kit (WLK) and separated from WDK.

See also

- Windows Driver Model
- Windows Logo Kit

External links

- Windows Driver Kit home page [2]

References

[1] http://www.microsoft.com/whdc/devtools/wdk/default.mspx

Windows Logo Kit

Developer(s)	Microsoft
Stable release	1.5
Development status	Active
Operating system	Windows
Platform	Windows
Available in	English
Website	[1]

The **Windows Logo Kit** (WLK) is a test automation framework provided by Microsoft to certify devices for Windows.

It provides automated scheduling and execution of the driver tests that hardware vendors are required to pass in order to qualify to use the Microsoft Designed for Windows Logo. It also enables users to automate driver tests they have created themselves. These tests can be mixed and matched with the Logo tests provided by Microsoft to create a custom test pass, which enables organizations to use the DTM to validate drivers in any way they see fit.

History of Windows Logo Kit

During the Windows 2000, XP, 2003 timeframe there was an old tool **Hardware Compatibility Test** (HCT) to certify devices. When Windows Vista was released the tool was replaced by **Driver Test Manager** (DTM) which can certify drivers for all then-supported platforms. At that time DTM was part of Windows Driver Kit (WDK). Later DTM was separated from WDK and changed to its current name, Windows Logo Kit.

Latest Version Of windows Logo Kit

The latest version of windows logo kit available is WLK1.5

See also

- Inquisitor — free/open-source hardware testing framework.
- WHQL Testing — Windows Hardware Quality Labs testing.

External links

- Windows Logo Kit home page [1]

References

[1] http://www.microsoft.com/whdc/winlogo/wlk/default.mspx

X00

X00 was a popular DOS-based FOSSIL driver[1] which was commonly used in the mid 1980s to the late 1990s and is even still used today. FOSSIL drivers were mainly used to run BBS software under MS-DOS. X00 can also be run under Windows, or even Linux and DOSEMU environments, to allow FOSSIL-aware MS-DOS based applications to function.

X00 was developed by Raymond L. Gwinn[1] from 1989 until 1993. The final release version was version 1.50, with a later beta version 1.53 which added support for baud rates above 38400. X00 is free for non-commercial usage. X00 included many enhancements to the FTC FOSSIL revision 5 specifications, which were later used in other FOSSIL drivers such as ADF and NetFoss.

Gwinn moved on to develop a replacement serial port driver for OS/2 called SIO. SIO contained a virtualized FOSSIL (VX00) that could be loaded if applications needed FOSSIL support.

References

[1] Raymond L. Gwinn (1990-07-15). "Functions reference manual for the X00 developer" (http://www.dcllabs.net/docs/x00ref.txt). DCL Labs. . Retrieved 2009-12-15.

Xpeak

Xpeak is an standard for device management, based on XML and platform agnostic, initially focused on financial applications but not restricted to it. It serves the same purpose that other APIs like CEN/XFS and J/XFS but is not restricted to one operating system or language, since it works in a client/server model using XML in a way to homogenise the communication between the application and the device services. It's flexibility allows different parts of the whole business to be implemented in different languages, having the application and the various devices, some implemented in Java, other in C++ and still others in the device's firmware.

It was designed based on the experiences had with CEN/XFS, J/XFS and JavaPOS, but instead of using an standards organization it uses and open source model to develop the architecture and tools used by the project, like it's base the complete open source software solution named Xpeaker. This way it can be updated, quickly and openly, by the users themselves, using the Internet as the means of communication rather than meetings requiring a physical presence.

Xpeak follows the open source model and participation in the project is totally free, but it is moderated by the R&D Open Source Foundation[1] , participated in equal parts by Sun Microsystems and Intecna[2] . The initial code contribution is the responsibility of Cashware[3] , one of the leading companies in devices connectivity through the use of standards (CEN/XFS and J/XFS).

Xpeaker

Xpeaker is a collection of software projects, integrally developed by Cashware, with the philosophy of Open Source and commercialized under a dual license the XPEAKER PUBLIC LICENSE and a commercial licence. Xpeaker includes the following elements:

Xpeaker IDE

An Eclipse Plugin which permits:

- Tests on the devices compatible with Xpeak to be carried out.
- Designs Forms
- Deployment
- Shares code

Xpeaker Services

Made up of:

- A set of basic classes for the development of Xpeak Services in Java.
- A collection of real device Services, including cash dispensers and recyclers, card readers, cheque readers, printers, bar code readers, etc.

Xpeaking

High level API for access to Xpeak Services. Xpeaking permits access to said services from different programming languages (Java, C, C++, C#, Pascal)

External links

- Xpeak Home Page [3]
- Documentation on Xpeaker Installation [4]
- Xpeaking for Java Examples [5]

References

[1] R&D Open Source Foundation web site (http://www.fidesol.org/)
[2] Intecna web site (http://www.intecna.es/)
[3] Cashware website (http://www.cashware.biz/)
[4] http://www.xpeak.org/documentation/xpeaker/XpeakerInstallation.pdf
[5] http://www.xpeak.org/documentation/xpeaker/XpeakingExamples.zip

Article Sources and Contributors

Filter driver *Source*: http://en.wikipedia.org/w/index.php?oldid=332213340 *Contributors*: Bluemoose, Condem, Frap, Lightdarkness, Soumyasch, Warren, WickWax, 4 anonymous edits

Microsoft Windows *Source*: http://en.wikipedia.org/w/index.php?oldid=373656073 *Contributors*: -Majestic-, 03jmgibbens, 1(), 16@r, 1nt2, 2mcm, 2toy mora, 62.253.64.xxx, 67773732TYU, 68DANNY2, 9ms, A Raider Like Indiana, A gnome, A-giau, ACCOM2222, Abhishikt, AbsoluteFlatness, Academic Challenger, Acroterion, Adam Mirowski, Adamacious, Adamodell, Admin@pcrevs.com, Ae-a, Aeæ, Afro Article, Ageha Winds, Ahodacsek, Ahoerstemeier, Aidan W, Aido2002, Aihtdikh, AimalCool, Ajm81, Akamad, Akhristov, Akira-otomo, Aksi great, Albert0057, Aldie, Alegoo92, Alemily, Alfio, AlistairMcMillan, Allstarecho, Almafeta, Althepal, Am088, Amcfreely, Amrykid, Andre Engels, Andrevan, Andrewtechhelp, Andros 1337, Andy16666, Andyh2, Angeljon121, Ann Stouter, Anog, Anonymous Dissident, Anonymous56789, Antandrus, Anthall1991, Antimatter15, Antique Rose, Anville, Anþony, Aomarks, Aqair, Aranel, Arch dude, Archer3, Archivist, Arnoldkul, Arthena, Ashdurbat, AstroNomer, Astroview120mm, Aude, Audrius u, AussieLegend, AvantgardeMVC, Avenue, Avihut, Avocado27, Ayjay1545, Azrael Nightwalker, B, BNSF Man, BUzTeD, Badwolf2212, Bakery2k, Banes, Barrera marquez, Bartosz, Bbq man, Bbriggs1, Bdoserror, Beinsane, Ben-Zin, Benandorsqueaks, Benc, Berek, Bergsten, Betelgeuse, Bevo, Bhadani, Bibliomaniac15, Big Booger, BigCow, BillG, BillWSmithJr, Billyswong, Bimmerosx, Binsurf, Binzisimpsons, Bissinger, Blackanddarkness, Blackcats, Blakkandekka, Blaxthos, Bleakcomb, Blobglob, Blowdart, Blubberboy92, Blueforce4116, Bluestriker, Bo98, Bobo192, Bobwrit, Bogods, Boris Allen, BostonMA, Boylett, Brandizzi, Brandon Brown, Brian0918, BrianGo28, BrianRecchia, Brianski, Brisvegas, BrokenSegue, Bubba hotep, Buchanan-Hermit, Buddha24, Burntsauce, CRFWNY, Cacophony, Caffelice, Caltas, Camembert, Can't sleep, clown will eat me, Canadian-Bacon, Candamir, Candorwien, CanisRufus, Caper13, CaptainVindaloo, Casper2k3, Cayindra, Cbrown1023, Cburnett, Ceeon, Celestra, CesarB, Ceyockey, Cff12345, Cgnabod, Cgs, Charles Gaudette, Charles dye, Chazz, Chille, Chmpoure, Chocolatemilk94, Chowbok, Chris 73, Chris Pickett, Chris the speller, Christian List, Chriswoz, Ciao 90, CitronManden, Cityscape4, Cjcamilla, Cjordan93, ClockworkTroll, Cnccccr, Codificate, Codyblevins, Coffee, Colin Hill, Cometstyles, Commander Keane, Computer boy2, Computerdan000, ConCompS, Coniosis, Conman23456, Conversion script, Coolcaesar, CoolingGibbon, Corporal clegg48, Cp111, Cpiral, Crazycomputers, Crazyromo, Crem23, Cremepuff222, Cristan, Crpietschmann, Cryptic, Cstanners, Ctbolt, Cuvtixo, Cvinoth, Cwolfsheep, Cyktsui, Cynical, Cyrius, D, D thadd, DHN, DOHC Holiday, DaDrumBum, DalekClock, Damian Yerrick, Dan D. Ric, Daniel5127, DanielRigal, Danny Beaudoin, DarkFalls, DarkHorizon, Darranc, Darremon, Darthnader37, Dasani, DataMatrix, Databases, Davelane, David Biddulph, David Gerard, David1409, Davidjk, Dcandeto, Dcolvin, Deanhowell123, Debackerl, Deeahbz, Dehumanizer, Delirium, Delldot, Deltabeignet, Demmy, Denniss, Derek Parnell, Deryck Chan, Dethomas, Deus2, Dieboybun, Diegogrez, Digita, DigitalLife, Dimre01, Dina, Dinjired, DinosaursLoveExistence, Disorganisation Man, Dj789, Djegan, Djhybrid117, Djmasala, Dmerrill, DmitryKo, Dog1818, Dojarca, Dolphinn, Downloaddude1258, Dp462090, Dragar Gt, Dragon 280, DragonflySixtyseven, Dragonhelmuk, Dstln, Dtech, Dudesleeper, Dungodung, Dust Filter, Dustin gayler, Dwheeler, Dysprosia, Dzubint, EH74DK, Eagleal, EatMyShortz, Ed g2s, Edgar181, Edgarde, EdgeOfEpsilon, Eelamstylez77, Eggsacute, Egil, El Dominio, Elassint, Eliotwiki, ElliotAdderton, Ellmist, Elm-39, Eloquence, Emacsuser, Enco1984, Enigmaaaaa, Enno, Enochlau, Ente75, Ergosteur, Esanchez7587, Escape Orbit, Evice, Evil Monkey, Evil saltine, Evosoho, Ewlyahoocom, Exodite, F.A.I.T.H.L.E.S.S, F80, FF2010, FaisaLakeel, Faithlessthewonderboy, Falco McCloud, Fantasy, Faradayplank, FatalError, Fatjoe151, FayssalF, Fbv65edel, Fdp, Felipe Aira, Ferkelparade, Ffx, Fiskegalen92, Fitzebwoy, Fiver2552, Flamurai, Flanakin, Flash200, FleetCommand, Flying Bishop, FlyingPenguins, Foo1995, Fowl2, FrancoGG, Frap, Fraslet, Freakofnurture, Frecklefoot, Fred Bradstadt, Frederik.Questier, FreeKresge, Freeeekyyy, Frenchman113, FreplySpang, FrozenPurpleCube, Frozenport, Fuck You, Funandtrvl, Furrykef, Fuzheado, GDonato, GNUtoo, GSK, Gadfium, Gaius Cornelius, Galactor213, Galoubet, Galwhaa, GamerXp, Gamerzworld, Gaming&Computing, Ganeshotaku, Ganfon, Gang65, Gaodifan, Gardar Rurak, Gary King, Gary Kirk, Gazpacho, Geek45, Geoffspear, George Adam Horváth, Georgia guy, Geraki, Gerbrant, Ghettoblaster, Gilbertogm, Gilliam, Glen, Gnepets, Goatasaur, Gogo Dodo, Goldom, Googler459, Googlesucks56789, Gosub, Graham87, GrandPoohBah, Grayshi, Grin, Grm wnr, Groggy Dice, Gronky, Grunt, Gscshoyru, Gtdp, Gunnar Guðvarðarson, Gustyfalcon, Guy Harris, Guyjohnston, Haakon, Haeleth, Hahafatpeople, Hairchrm, Hall Monitor, Halsteadk, Hammersoft, Happenstance, Harryboyles, Haseo9999, Hbomb phd mom, Hdt83, Heapchk, Hebrides, Helixblue, Hello32020, Hendrixski, Henry W. Schmitt, HereToHelp, Hirosho, Holbred, Howardjp, Hungupbg, Hurtstotalktoyou, Husky, Hydr, Hypnoticcyst, I8189720, IGod, ILOVELOL32, IMSoP, IXella007, Iain99, Ian Pitchford, Ianjones50, Illegal Operation, Illyria05, Ilya, IlyaHaykinson, Ilyanep, Indefatigable, Indon, Injust, Interframe, Ioprwe, Ipodsocool, Iridescent, ItsProgrammable, Ivan Pozdeev, Ixfd64, J Di, JCarriker, JIP, JLaTondre, JWSchmidt, JYOuyang, JYolkowski, Jacob Hnri 5, JacquesStrap, Jaericho, Jake Wasdin, James Michael 1, Jamieostrich, Jan Hofmann, Jauerback, Jaxl, Jcbparry, Jcurtin, Jdlowery, Jdm64, Jeffwang16, Jeremy Visser, JeremyA, Jerryseinfeld, Jerrysmp, Jesse Viviano, Jesus5555, Jesus764, Jesuss, JettaMann, Jevel66, Jiffy, Jigs41793, Jimmi Hugh, Jimothytrotter, Jimthing, Jiy, Jketola, Jkonline, Jmath666, Jmjglick, Jmoynihan08hm77, JoJan, JoThousand, Joanjoc, JoanneB, Joejoejo, Joffeloff, Johann Wolfgang, John, John Ericson, John Goettle, JohnOwens, Johnclow13, Johnleemk, Johnmc, Johnuniq, Jojit fb, Jon vs, JonasL, Jonatan Swift, Jondel, Jonghyunchung, Jopxton, Jordan015, Josh the Nerd, Joshua Issac, JoshuaArgent, Joyous!, Jpoke89, Jrcure, Jsmethers, Jtc, Ju66l3r, JuJube, JuanC08, Julian Mendez, Jumbo Snails, Justanother, Jyoz, Kakomu, Kar.ma, Karimarie, Karnesky, Kaycubs, Kaysov, Kbh3rd, Kbolino, Kelly Martin, Kesla, Kevinkor2, Keyser Söze, Khym Chanur, Kierenj, Kigali1, KingpinE7, Kinneyboy90, Kipholbeck, Kissmeplease, Kjhonsa, Kkm010, Klingoncowboy4, KnowledgeOfSelf, Knutux, Kohlmalo, Kolonuk, Korossyl, Kozuch, KrakatoaKatie, Krawi, Kungfuadam, Kungming2, Kurieeto, Kwen, La goutte de pluie, Lacrimosus, Lahiru k, Lantay77, Larry laptop, Lbs6380, Lcarsdata, LeadSpeaker, Leandrod, Lectonar, LeeHunter, Leif, Leithp, LeoNomis, Letdorf, Leuko, Liberty Miller, Lightmouse, Linear88, Linuxbeak, Linuxerist, LionKimbro, Llalala, Localzuk, Lonaowna, LonelyBeacon, Lookslikesiterent, Lou.weird, Lowellian, Luce007, Luk, Lumpbucket, Luna Santin, Lupin, M Johnson, MADCastro2012, MCC, MER-C, MERC, MJGR, MK8, MMMEEE, MZMcBride, Ma8thew, Mac, MacGeekGuy, Madcow 93, Maester mensch, Magister Mathematicae, Mailer diablo, Malo, Man123123, Marceki111, Marcok, Mark, Mark85296341, MarkGallagher, MarkSpearmint, Markhurd, Markie2, Martarius, Martyx, Marudubshinki, Marx Gomes, Marysunshine, Massysett, MasterCole, Mastershake86, Mathwizxp, Matt Crypto, Mattarata, Mav, Max Schwarz, Maxim Masiutin, Maximus Rex, McLovin34, Mcwatson, Meelar, MehranVB, Mephiles602, Metalim, Methanegas, Metz2000, Mguy77, Mgw854, Michael Angelkovich, Michael Ray, Michaeldadmum, Michaelpremsrirat, Midgrid, Midkay, Mike4ty4, MikeZuniga, Mild Bill Hiccup, Milfman, Minesweeper, MinorItem, Mithent, Mjpieters, Mkdw, Mlscdi, Mmoll21m, Mms, Mo0, Modster, Monedula, MontyB, Moonknightus, Moonridersaregay, Moonwolf14, Mr Bartels, Mr. Lefty, Mr. XYZ, Mrdelayer, Ms2ger, Mugunth Kumar, Mulad, Mushroom, Mvmarier, Mwtoews, Mxn, Myanw, Nachmore, Naddy, Naltrexone, Nanshu, NapoliRoma, Nathan nfm, Nathanlilienthal13, Neelchauhan, Neo2256, NewGuy4, Newfraferz87, Nick2253, Nimc, Nintendog master 54, Nishkid64, Nixdorf, Njan, Nmnmnm, Noypi380, Nukleartoaster, Nurg, O, Odd bloke, Off!, Okwestern, OlEnglish, Olioster, Ollie the Magic Skater, Omicronpersei8, Ondrejsv, Oneupthextraman, Opagecrtr, Opelio, OregonD00d, Oscarthecat, Ost316, OtherPerson, OwenX, Oxymoron83, Ozherb, PPGMD, Packard Bell Legend, Padsquad43, Pakaran, Patrick, Patrickweeks007, Patrolman89, Paul Cyr, Paul Stansifer, Paulfp, Pavel Vozenilek, Persian Poet Gal, Petaluma Paranormal, Peter Grey, Peteturtle, Petrwiki, Peyman4u, Peyre, Pgiii, Pgk, Phanton, Phil Sandifer, Philip Trueman, Pigman, PileOnades, Pinikas, Piratesmack, Plugwash, Pokyrek, Poor Yorick, Poweroid, Prolog, Propound, Pschulz01, PsyMar, Pursey, QUAZWRATH, Qudder, Quinsareth, Quoladdie, Qwerty124gg, Qwitchibo, Qxl32, Qxz, RB972, RN, RTC, RadioActive, Radon210, Raja99, Ramanpotential, RandomP, Rasmasyean, Rbuj, Rchamberlain, Rcmouse1010, Rd syringe, Rderijcke, Rdsmith4, Reallikeunreal, Rebecca, Rebroad, Red Dalek, Red Director, RedKlonoa, RedXII, Redvers, Reilly, Reisio, Remember the dot, Repetition, Resplendent, RevolverOcelotX, Rhesusmonkeyboy, Rhobite, Rhtc, Rich Farmbrough, Richard Lotspard, Richard626, Ricjl, RickK, Riluve, Rjecina, Rjwilmsi, Rlevse, Roadrunnah, Robartin, Robbie940, Robert Buzink, Robert H, Robert Xia, RobertG, Robertd, Robinhw, Rocastelo, Rocket71048576, Rockymountains, Rodeo90, Roketjack, RolandH, Ronark, Rsantmann, Rsm99833, Running, Rursus, Rutherfordjigsaw, Ruud Koot, Rwwww, Ryan Postlethwaite, Ryan t moua, S0aasdf2sf, SF007, SHARD, SHeumann, SNIyer12, ST47, SYSS Mouse, Sam Hocevar, Samuel, Samuel Blanning, Samvscat, Sango123, Sasquatch, Sauronjim, Scepia, SchmuckyTheCat, SchuminWeb, Science4sail, Scientus, Scifiintel, Sciurinæ, Scorpiona, Scottymoze, Scriberius, Scuiqui fox, SeanMack, Sebmathews, Sebrat, Secretlondon, Selfdiscipline, Selivanow, September 11 terrorist, Sethoeph, Sfan00 IMG, Shakumafu, Shandris, Shanes, Shashank Shekhar, Shelmac, Shibboleth, Shinjiman, Shnout, Sigma 7, Sigmundpetersen, Sikon, Silvergoat, SimonEast, SimonP, SimonTrew, Simxp, SirGrant, Siroxo, Sjakkalle, Sjorford, Skirks, Skiwi, Skyeap, Slashuer, Slathering, Sleepeeg3, Slipknotmetal, Smokizzy, SmoothNikola, Smurfy, Smyth, Snaxe920, Snoyes, SoSaysChappy, Solphusion, Somaditya, Somebody in the WWW, Soumyasch, Southpark20, Spe88, Spear of fire, Specter01010, SpeedyGonsales, Spencerperry, Sperling, Spliced, Spookfish, Spug, Srnelson, Ssd, Starionwolf, Steel, StephenH, Stephenchou0722, SteveRwanda, Stevenh123, Stevietheman, Stilroc, Stino v, Stonda, StuIsCool, StuThomas, Supers, Supremeknowledge, Suruena, SusanLesch, Susvolans, Swabjob, Sweetback, Swollib, Swotboy2000, SyntaxError55, Synthiss, Szhang21, TAG.Odessa, TJ Spyke, Ta bu shi da yu, Tacvek, Tadas12, TakuyaMurata, Tangotango, Tannin, Tarashav, Tawker, Teamcritical, Tech2blog, Techman224, Techmdrn, Template namespace initialisation script, Tepidpond, Terence, TerrenceandPhillip, Tfgbd, Thaek, Thalakan, Thavian, The Colclough, The Disco Times, The Epopt, The Fish, The Geneticist, The Rambling Man, The wub, TheChrisD, TheDoober, TheKMan, TheNewPhobia, ThePointblank, Thealexweb, Theazman1, Thegreenj, Thetehror, Thewallowmaker, Thewikipedian, Thingg, Think outside the box, This, that and the other, Thisisntfake1, Thomas H. Larsen, Thompson.matthew, Thorpe, Throup, Thu, Thumperward, TiCPU, Tiggerjay, TimR, Timmeh, Timwi, Tinton5, ToasterOS, Tomcage9, Tomi Undergallows, Tommy Irianto, Tompagenet, Tonsofpcs, Tony1, Tothwolf, Towel401, Towsonu2003, Toyotaboy95, Treekids, Tregoweth, TrekMaster, Trevor MacInnis, Tripacer99, Trivialist, Trusilver, Tsunaminoai, Ttwaring, TubularWorld, TuneyLoon, Turionaltec, TuukkaH, Twernt, Tyomitch, Tyraios, UMC2, Uli, Ultimus, Umofomia, Unimaginative Username, Unknownperson1234, Uriel8, Utcursch, Vahid83, Vbrtrmn, Vedek Dukat, Vegaswikian, Vincent.premysler, Vontafeijos, Wackymacs, Walter Görlitz, WalterGR, Wanderson9, Wangmike, Wapcaplet, Warlordwolf, Warren, Wengier, Werdan7, Werideatdusk33, Whiteford8, Whkoh, Widefox, Wiki alf, Wiki fanatic, WikiBone, WikiFew, WikiMan44, Wikinger, WikipedianMarlith, Wikiwaka101, Windowsknowitall@msn.com, WindowzRULZlolZ, Windsok, Wknight94, Wlklpedla is meant to be vandalized, Wmahan, Wmplayer, Wow1000, Wykis, X1987x, XJamRastafire, Xation, Xelgen, Xeysz, Xgmx, Ximian99, Xlation, Xmachina, Xp54321, Xpclient, XrXeJoeXaXpXeXr, Xtreme racer, Xtremerandomness, YUL89YYZ, Yama, Yamamoto Ichiro, Yamla, Yasirniazkhan, Yeeshenhao, Yergizmo, Ynhockey, Yousifnet, Yuckfoo, Yuhong, Z.E.R.O., Z98, ZFU738, Zakfleming, Zapvet, Zeeboid, Zepheus, Zntrip, Zondor, Zoney, Zundark, , 乌尔奇奥拉, 每日飞龙, 1494 anonymous edits

Windows Driver Model *Source*: http://en.wikipedia.org/w/index.php?oldid=370667098 *Contributors*: Akhristov, Aldie, AlistairMcMillan, AndreR908, Arny, BWCNY, Bongle, Cwolfsheep, DabMachine, Davewho2, Digita, Ericd, FcxSanya, Feedmecereal, Grvasu, Ham Pastrami, HappyDog, Imroy, Jdb67usa, Jerome Charles Potts, JohnOwens, Leeor net, Lofote, Minesweeper, OS2Warp, Omegatron, Phatom87, PhilipMW, Rjwilmsi, Soumyasch, Ta bu shi da yu, Totsugeki, Ttcmp, Warren, Wik, Xpclient, Yukoba, 51 anonymous edits

Device Driver *Source*: http://en.wikipedia.org/w/index.php?oldid=174845872 *Contributors*: 63.117.239.xxx, AVRS, Adamhollick, Alansohn, Aldie, AlistairMcMillan, Anabus, Anaxial, Andareed, Andre Engels, Andy16666, Angela, Apparition11, Attilios, Aurista25, Avkulkarni, Awaterl, Aweiredguy, Ayla, BMF81, BMT, Babajobu, Bbx, BenFrantzDale, Beno1000, Bevo, Bhadani, Biscuittin, Bobo192, Borgx, Btilm, COMPFUNK2, CanisRufus, Capricorn42, Ched Davis, ChrisJMoor, Classical Esther, Cometstyles, Conversion script, Cool3, DMCer, Da Joe, Damieng, Davehi1, David Edgar, Diego Moya, Dispensa, Doctahdrey, Dragon Dan, El C, Elsendero, Endlessnameless, Enjoi4586, Equatorian, Equendil, Erdeee, Fabartus, FatalError, Frap, Fsgeek, Fæ, GRAHAMUK, Gbeuk99, Gilbertgagnon, Glenn, Gragox, Greenrd, Haiviet, Harumphy, HenryLi, Herakleitoszefesu, Hu12, Iakjfhfuksn, Ich, Imroy, Itsluy, JTN, Jane Fairfax, Jetwhiz, Jorunn, Josepant, Joshuamarius, Justin545, Kbrose, Kenny sh, Kerdek, Knownot, Knutux, Kozuch, Krótki, Kurykh, Kvng, Kyng, Laurusnobilis, Leejjcn, Lightmouse, MER-C, Mac, Macar, Mboverload, Mhaitham.shammaa, Mickraus, Mipadi, Mirror Vax, Mjuarez, Nacase, Nickols k, Nixdorf, Nopetro, Norborb, NuclearWinner, Ok.book.guy, Oswazteca, Oxymoron83, Ozzmosis,

Pablo-flores, Paul Richter, Perspective, Pgan002, Pgk, Phatom87, PhilipO, Piano non troppo, Pietrozuco, Quux, R'n'B, R4f, Raven4x4x, Reddi, Remember the dot, Renoj, Rich Farmbrough, Rilak, Rjwilmsi, Romanm, RossPatterson, SF007, Seidenstud, Seishirou Sakurazuka, ShakespeareFan00, Silvonen, Socrates2008, Sohchouhan, Spiko-carpediem, Stephenb, Steven Weston, StuartBrady, Technobadger, Tedickey, The Red, The Thing That Should Not Be, Thumperward, Trekkie4christ, UncleDouggie, Uriyan, Warren, Wayiran, WegianWarrior, Wikiklrsc, Winterst, Wk muriithi, Yakudza, Yamaguchi先生, Ysangkok, Yukoba, Yworo, ZimZalaBim, Zzuuzz, ^demon, ترجمان05, 285 anonymous edits

Advanced Configuration and Power Interface *Source*: http://en.wikipedia.org/w/index.php?oldid=373066694 *Contributors*: Abdull, Aldie, Alison, Altonbr, Andrewpmk, Angela, Autopilot, Avocade, BD2412, Bajasren13, Bggoldie, Bissinger, Bluemonkey15, Borgx, Brandon, Bschoeni, CanisRufus, Carbuncle, CesarB, Chealer, Chicarelli, Conversion script, Craigm71, Ctimko, Daniel.Cardenas, Daredevilnut123, Deiz, Dogcow, Dr unix, DragonHawk, Dsf7183, EagleOne, Edyu, Electron9, Emacsuser, Eptin, Favonian, Fragglet, Frap, Frau Holle, FreeRangeFrog, FreelanceWizard, Gaius Cornelius, Gardar Rurak, Geheimdienst, Geimas5, General Wesc, Goffrie, Goodone121, Gribeco, Hawk777, Hulvey, II MusLiM HyBRiD II, Inclusivedisjunction, Intgr, Jboyles, Jec, Jengelh, Jesse Viviano, Jimmi Hugh, Jm51, Jobbon, JorgePeixoto, Joriki, Jsmethers, Jtatum, Judzillah, KDesk, Kbolino, Kostmo, Kozuch, Lavenderbunny, Lcrosetto, Letdorf, Lincoln.max, LionsPhil, M1ss1ontomars2k4, Mac, Marshall Williams2, Mboverload, Meisam, Michael2, MilchFlasche, Mirror Vax, Monedula, Myrmornis, Nik-Hill, Nikerabbit, Nile, Nixdorf, Nuno Tavares, Oli Filth, Paolocos, Phunehehe, Pit, Plasma, Posix memalign, Riluve, Sam8, Savant13, SchmuckyTheCat, Shellreef, SimonP, Sj, Slatedorg, Snarius, Someguy1221, Sourcejedi, Spoon!, StanfordProgrammer, Superbignerd, Ta bu shi da yu, Technorj, The Anome, TiCPU, Tobias Bergemann, Todd Vierling, TomBattle, Trasz, Tuxisuau, UMC2, Warren, WatchAndObserve, Wernher, Widefox, William Graham, Winterst, WojPob, X!, Xiaomao101, Yuhong, Zodon, 181 anonymous edits

Device driver *Source*: http://en.wikipedia.org/w/index.php?oldid=369481698 *Contributors*: 63.117.239.xxx, AVRS, Adamhollick, Alansohn, Aldie, AlistairMcMillan, Anabus, Anaxial, Andareed, Andre Engels, Andy16666, Angela, Apparition11, Attilios, Aurista25, Avkulkarni, Awaterl, Aweiredguy, Ayla, BMF81, BMT, Babajobu, Bbx, BenFrantzDale, Beno1000, Bevo, Bhadani, Biscuittin, Bobo192, Borgx, Btilm, COMPFUNK2, CanisRufus, Capricorn42, Ched Davis, ChrisJMoor, Classical Esther, Cometstyles, Conversion script, Cool3, DMCer, Da Joe, Damieng, Davehi1, David Edgar, Diego Moya, Dispensa, Doctahdrey, Dragon Dan, El C, Elsendero, Endlessnameless, Enjoi4586, Equatorian, Equendil, Erdeee, Fabartus, FatalError, Frap, Fsgeek, Fæ, GRAHAMUK, Gbeuk99, Gilbertgagnon, Glenn, Gragox, Greenrd, Haiviet, Harumphy, HenryLi, Herakleitoszefesu, Hu12, Iakjfhfuksn, Ich, Imroy, Itsluy, JTN, Jane Fairfax, Jetwhiz, Jorunn, Josepant, Joshuamarius, Justin545, Kbrose, Kenny sh, Kerdek, Knownot, Knutux, Kozuch, Krótki, Kurykh, Kvng, Kyng, Laurusnobilis, Leejjcn, Lightmouse, MER-C, Mac, Macar, Mboverload, Mhaitham.shammaa, Mickraus, Mipadi, Mirror Vax, Mjuarez, Nacase, Nickols k, Nixdorf, Nopetro, Norborb, NuclearWinner, Ok.book.guy, Oswazteca, Oxymoron83, Ozzmosis, Pablo-flores, Paul Richter, Perspective, Pgan002, Pgk, Phatom87, PhilipO, Piano non troppo, Pietrozuco, Quux, R'n'B, R4f, Raven4x4x, Reddi, Remember the dot, Renoj, Rich Farmbrough, Rilak, Rjwilmsi, Romanm, RossPatterson, SF007, Seidenstud, Seishirou Sakurazuka, ShakespeareFan00, Silvonen, Socrates2008, Sohchouhan, Spiko-carpediem, Stephenb, Steven Weston, StuartBrady, Technobadger, Tedickey, The Red, The Thing That Should Not Be, Thumperward, Trekkie4christ, UncleDouggie, Uriyan, Warren, Wayiran, WegianWarrior, Wikiklrsc, Winterst, Wk muriithi, Yakudza, Yamaguchi先生, Ysangkok, Yukoba, Yworo, ZimZalaBim, Zzuuzz, ^demon, ترجمان05, 285 anonymous edits

ATI Catalyst *Source*: http://en.wikipedia.org/w/index.php?oldid=372736693 *Contributors*: 16@r, AMD64, Babakz, Capricorn42, Chluk2425, Colbuckshot, Crt, Crystallina, DarkRadeon, Darkuranium, Fiftyquid, GoddersUK, Ham Pastrami, Kozuch, LOL, Leofric1, Loompyloompy313, Mewtu, Mwiersma, Nancy, Oldag07, Phoenix-forgotten, Playwrite, Rhe br, Ronark, Rossi27530, Salam32, Silvergoat, Skyhawker666, Svetovid, Typhoon87, Wiak, Xhin, 56 anonymous edits

Advanced SCSI Programming Interface *Source*: http://en.wikipedia.org/w/index.php?oldid=340901068 *Contributors*: Alecv, Anon lynx, Episteme-jp, Eras-mus, Everyking, Frap, Glenfarclas, Helix84, Kbdank71, Liftarn, MarchHare, Marcika, Mirror Vax, Möbius27, Nixeagle, Rich Farmbrough, Sandstein, Sbonds, Sdrtirs, Spikey, T chan3819, The Anome, Vina, Voidvector, Zoe, 28 anonymous edits

Airjack (device driver) *Source*: http://en.wikipedia.org/w/index.php?oldid=350570016 *Contributors*: Biscuittin, Dawynn, Dwaipayan Dutta, JaGa, 1 anonymous edits

BNU (software) *Source*: http://en.wikipedia.org/w/index.php?oldid=301683826 *Contributors*: AVRS, Frap, Fyuanster, Gay Cdn, Hughcharlesparker, JarlaxleArtemis, Pcmicro, Psychonaut, Tan90deg, Twas Now, Wkitty42, 1 anonymous edits

Broadcast Driver Architecture *Source*: http://en.wikipedia.org/w/index.php?oldid=333386310 *Contributors*: CX23882-19, Cyzor, KelleyCook, MNewnham, Miami33139, Pegship, Retired username, Roberthunt, Starbois, Tanger, TimSE, Warren, 22 anonymous edits

CEN/XFS *Source*: http://en.wikipedia.org/w/index.php?oldid=360244534 *Contributors*: Akhristov, Anton14, Betacommand, Bruno.schmidt, Chowbok, Cwolfsheep, Gaius Cornelius, HW001, Intgr, Kathleen.wright5, Maribert, MartinMarcher, PrimroseGuy, R Math, SCEhardt, Soumyasch, TMC1221, Timo Honkasalo, 51 anonymous edits

Class driver *Source*: http://en.wikipedia.org/w/index.php?oldid=240224098 *Contributors*: CamTarn, Frap, GRAHAMUK, J Di, JonHarder, Snori, 5 anonymous edits

CUPS *Source*: http://en.wikipedia.org/w/index.php?oldid=369559496 *Contributors*: Aervanath, Ahoerstemeier, Ahunt, Airblaine, Alai, AlistairMcMillan, Analoguedragon, Antandrus, Ascánder, Audiocow, Bobblewik, Bookandcoffee, Bovineone, Bozoid, Brisvegas, Bruce89, Burgundavia, CFeyecare, Cabhan, CanisRufus, Chealer, ChrisCork, Cliffb, ConradPino, CyberSkull, Daev, Davis080, Dbenbenn, Demonuk, Dismas, Dysprosia, EAi, Edupedro, Edward, Eequor, Eldarin, EmielMols, Fatmanlarry, Finbarr Saunders, Gardar Rurak, Gcbirzan, Ghepeu, Giraffedata, GoodOmens, Graue, Gronky, Gskuse, Guy Harris, Guzhogi, Gürkan Sengün, Hadal, Hairy Dude, Hansjorn, Harumphy, Hawaiian717, Hogrix, Improv, IrisKawling, Itai, Japsu, Jdavidb, Jhartmann, JohnWhitlock, Juansempere, Julesd, KDesk, KSmrq, Kaszeta, Kl4m-AWB, Kozuch, Linuxerist, Ljhenshall, Localzuk, Lomn, Lupin, Mac, Madd the sane, Mairi, Malleus Fatuorum, MarekMahut, MarkSweep, Market, Marskell, Massysett, Metallicradiation428, MinorContributor, Mirror Vax, Morte, Mpj17, Mushroom, Nealmcb, Nikai, Nufy8, Oblivious, OverlordQ, PGSONIC, Paul A, Pkirlin, PleaseStand, Plek, Polluks, Popelin, Printman, Project FMF, Prolog, Quarl, Qwertyus, Reub2000, Rjwilmsi, Rollerjack25, SF007, Samsara, SandyGeorgia, Schneelocke, SecVortex, Sfisher, Silsor, SirGrant, Smihael, Sparklex, Speaker to Lampposts, Stassats, Ta bu shi da yu, Thincat, Thiseye, Thumperward, Thunderbrand, Tomwalden, Tony1, Tonybrown100, Tothwolf, Trixx, Ww, Xaosflux, Xueshengyao, Yomangani, Ævar Arnfjörð Bjarmason, 167 anonymous edits

DOCS (software) *Source*: http://en.wikipedia.org/w/index.php?oldid=313763522 *Contributors*: Jake Wartenberg, M-le-mot-dit, UnicornTapestry, 4 anonymous edits

DirectX Video Acceleration *Source*: http://en.wikipedia.org/w/index.php?oldid=371205458 *Contributors*: Akata, Danielulfe, Dravecky, Gamester17, Intgr, JLaTondre, Kengelha, Kentyman, KnownIssues, Malept, Miami33139, N1cholson, Odo1982, Regression Tester, RodolfoVargas, Ruud Koot, Sladen, Soumyasch, VodkaJazz, Voidvector, Warren, Wolfsoft, XanderJ, Xpclient, 64 anonymous edits

Driver Verifier *Source*: http://en.wikipedia.org/w/index.php?oldid=323435985 *Contributors*: Ngyikp, Tuxplorer, Warren

F6 disk *Source*: http://en.wikipedia.org/w/index.php?oldid=372818019 *Contributors*: Biscuittin, Colonies Chris, Frap, GSMR, GermanX, Reswobslc, Top Cat, 14 anonymous edits

FreedomHEC *Source*: http://en.wikipedia.org/w/index.php?oldid=363941694 *Contributors*: Frap, Kozuch, Matthew Yeager, Moxfyre, Rjwilmsi

HostAP *Source*: http://en.wikipedia.org/w/index.php?oldid=357867817 *Contributors*: ArbiterOne, Daverocks, Frap, John94501, Kathleen.wright5, Majorly, Pandemias, Pmetzger, 11 anonymous edits

I/O request packet *Source*: http://en.wikipedia.org/w/index.php?oldid=351590059 *Contributors*: Jeh, Mephiles602, Soumyasch, Warren, Xpclient, Yutsi, Zappa711, 1 anonymous edits

IA-32 Execution Layer *Source*: http://en.wikipedia.org/w/index.php?oldid=365733459 *Contributors*: A5b, Arch dude, Brianski, David Gerard, Fisherjs, Frap, GregorB, Lenin and McCarthy, Maury Markowitz, Richardcavell, Tuxcantfly

J/XFS *Source*: http://en.wikipedia.org/w/index.php?oldid=355611415 *Contributors*: Bruno.schmidt, JLaTondre, 2 anonymous edits

Kernel-Mode Driver Framework *Source*: http://en.wikipedia.org/w/index.php?oldid=362772862 *Contributors*: BWCNY, Balabiot, Bongle, Frap, Manohars, Miamidot, N1cholson, Scott McNay, Soumyasch, Warren, Yuhong, Yukoba, 41 anonymous edits

Leaf driver *Source*: http://en.wikipedia.org/w/index.php?oldid=364559927 *Contributors*: BD2412, BirgitteSB, Boyanov, EagleFan, Galactiger, J04n, Paul A, Pegship, Robertvan1, Skier Dude, 2 anonymous edits

Mirror driver *Source*: http://en.wikipedia.org/w/index.php?oldid=366647788 *Contributors*: DanDare, Frap, Happywren, Limitedmage, Rjwilmsi, 3 anonymous edits

Mode-setting *Source*: http://en.wikipedia.org/w/index.php?oldid=365221678 *Contributors*: 1ForTheMoney, Fcrozat, Frap, Gang65, H2g2bob, Jojo 1, KDesk, Manuelciosici, MichiGreat, Milan Keršláger, Papa November, Reisio, Rpgdude, Unravelingthread, Widefox, 9 anonymous edits

NDISwrapper *Source*: http://en.wikipedia.org/w/index.php?oldid=371523488 *Contributors*: Brassett, Chealer, Crazycomputers, Cyde, DagErlingSmørgrav, Edward, Edwtie, Etienne.navarro, Ezeu, Faisal.akeel, Gtyron, Guy Harris, HDCase, JPLeRouzic, Jimbley, Jmorgan, Julian Andres Klode, Kaitocracy, Kycook, Linoox, LordOfer, Mac, Mareklug, Martinultima, Mild Bill Hiccup, MureninC, Napalm Llama, Novalis, OS2Warp, Optichan, Panyd, Peyre, Pgan002, Pipatron, Pmsyyz, Pol098, Raphael Frey, Rogerborg, SF007, Saurael, Smyth, SniperBeamer, StevenHidy, Stiepan Pietrov, Swirlix, Thumperward, Waldo the terrible, 59 anonymous edits

Nexus driver *Source*: http://en.wikipedia.org/w/index.php?oldid=240838024 *Contributors*: Boyanov, Dlh-stablelights, Frap, Paul A, Skier Dude, Tinucherian

Omega Drivers *Source*: http://en.wikipedia.org/w/index.php?oldid=369054885 *Contributors*: Cfslattery1, Corevette, Craig5320, Dungeonscaper, Emesee, Interiot, JKos12, Lordbal, Merope, Molnart, Pascal.Tesson, Pauli133, Personblue, Real NC, Slowking Man, Tombomp, Twas Now, 16 anonymous edits

PC/TCP Packet Driver *Source*: http://en.wikipedia.org/w/index.php?oldid=373057340 *Contributors*: Electron9, OlEnglish, RCX

Printer driver *Source*: http://en.wikipedia.org/w/index.php?oldid=348885696 *Contributors*: Abdull, AlistairMcMillan, Biscuittin, Bkil, CanisRufus, Chealer, Emperorbma, FF2010, Graham87, Iridescent, Itsluy, Iznikarius, MaverickSolutions, Minghong, Monedula, MushroomCloud, Naddy, Nida batool, Nixdorf, Nuttycoconut, Ohnoitsjamie, Phatom87, Pollinator, Polluks, R. S. Shaw, Raffaele Megabyte, RedWolf, Rlest, Rwxrwxrwx, Sam Hocevar, SkeletorUK, Spamus Aran, Steveprutz, Tedder, Vespristiano, Warren, 57 anonymous edits

SCSI Pass-Through Direct *Source*: http://en.wikipedia.org/w/index.php?oldid=361438570 *Contributors*: Andareed, Anon lynx, Cyrus XIII, DanielPharos, Devin122, Drw25, Frap, Jackie, JensRex, Joseph881, Macraig, Oldmankdude, Phatom87, Thealliedhacker, Uzume, Warren, 18 anonymous edits

SIO (software) *Source*: http://en.wikipedia.org/w/index.php?oldid=338311453 *Contributors*: 1ForTheMoney, AVRS, Christopher Kraus, InsufficientData, Rich Farmbrough, Wlindley, 4 anonymous edits

Scanner Access Now Easy *Source*: http://en.wikipedia.org/w/index.php?oldid=366117014 *Contributors*: Ahunt, Apoc2400, Baron1984, BioTube, Chealer, Cummins1, DanMS, Darkst, EagleOne, Electron9, Frap, Gurch, Imroy, JKD, Kate, Markus Kuhn, Mirror Vax, Rick Sidwell, Rjwilmsi, Romanc19s, SF007, Scarlet Lioness, Skamphausen, Somercet, Storkk, Ta bu shi da yu, Tedickey, Thorwald, Wafulz, WikiWikiPhil, Yworo, 26 anonymous edits

SciTech SNAP *Source*: http://en.wikipedia.org/w/index.php?oldid=337660350 *Contributors*: Jacob Poon, 4 anonymous edits

SCSI Pass Through Interface *Source*: http://en.wikipedia.org/w/index.php?oldid=340706821 *Contributors*: AnatolyVilchinsky, Anon lynx, Gaius Cornelius, Glenfarclas, Kbrose, Rror, Voidvector, 4 anonymous edits

Uniform Driver Interface *Source*: http://en.wikipedia.org/w/index.php?oldid=333692541 *Contributors*: Alynna Kasmira, Bookofjude, Electron9, Frap, Gmatic, Kesla, MarkMLl, Pascal.Tesson, Pegship, Suruena, That Guy, From That Show!, 10 anonymous edits

UniVBE *Source*: http://en.wikipedia.org/w/index.php?oldid=365648691 *Contributors*: Beckncall, Dro Kulix, Jacob Poon, Joe99soap, JonHarder, Krótki, Lavenderbunny, Mike Dallwitz, Pcb21, Sfan00 IMG, Swaaye, TanatOS, 1 anonymous edits

Universal Audio Architecture *Source*: http://en.wikipedia.org/w/index.php?oldid=284930572 *Contributors*: Abdull, Akhristov, Cwolfsheep, Ghettoblaster, Jesse Viviano, Lightdarkness, Mikeguz, Minkus, Soumyasch, Warren, Ww, Xpclient, 17 anonymous edits

User space *Source*: http://en.wikipedia.org/w/index.php?oldid=362499764 *Contributors*: Alvredeveld, Andrew625, Andy16666, Appleseed, BMF81, Beno1000, Borgx, Cgmusselman, Cybercobra, Damian Yerrick, Dazzla, Druiloor, Friviere, Gherald, H2g2bob, Intgr, Itai, Jerome Charles Potts, Joy, JulesH, Mac, Marioosz, Memming, Public Menace, Pythagoras1, R. S. Shaw, RainbowCrane, Rathee, Ron Ritzman, SkyWalker, Streissel, Tqbf, WODUP, 24 anonymous edits

User-Mode Driver Framework *Source*: http://en.wikipedia.org/w/index.php?oldid=362773995 *Contributors*: Alksub, BWCNY, Balabiot, Gerbrant, Imroy, Mboverload, Miamidot, Plm209, Soumyasch, Thegeneralguy, Themilan, Warren, Yukoba, 54 anonymous edits

Vidix *Source*: http://en.wikipedia.org/w/index.php?oldid=364017723 *Contributors*: Andreas Kaufmann, Calliopejen1, DanDare, Erbureth, Nickols k, PigFlu Oink, Rich Farmbrough, Thumperward, Wrk384, 5 anonymous edits

VxD *Source*: http://en.wikipedia.org/w/index.php?oldid=366845441 *Contributors*: Cwolfsheep, Derbeth, Equendil, Evercat, Fiftyquid, Frap, Ham Pastrami, Jed, Jesse Viviano, Jh51681, Jkl, JohnOwens, Josh the Nerd, KeKe, Modster, Nate Silva, Ohnoitsjamie, Phatom87, RTC, Rebroad, ShakespeareFan00, Shalom Yechiel, SoonerDub, Starionwolf, SteveLoughran, Tannin, Thumperward, Tim Starling, Tregoweth, Ttcmp, Tyomitch, Warren, WynCntry, Xpclient, Zoicon5, 33 anonymous edits

Windows Display Driver Model *Source*: http://en.wikipedia.org/w/index.php?oldid=373474363 *Contributors*: 1ForTheMoney, AbJ32, Achagl, AlistairMcMillan, Amire80, Ben b, Billy the Impaler, Canadacow, Cwolfsheep, Danwarne, DmitryKo, Fran z, Frap, Ghettoblaster, Heron, Ilion2, Jesse Viviano, Kenchikuben, Mr. XYZ, N1cholson, Naelphin, Nk, Petri Krohn, Rich Farmbrough, Rjwilmsi, Romanc19s, Seth ze, Shawnc, Sotcr, Soumyasch, Svick, Vektor330, Warren, Xpclient, YUL89YYZ, 87 anonymous edits

Windows Driver Foundation *Source*: http://en.wikipedia.org/w/index.php?oldid=369549060 *Contributors*: Akhristov, Alvin-cs, BWCNY, Bongle, DNTH8DarkSide, EmperorPsiblade, Escape Orbit, Iridescent, Jamelan, Luna Santin, Miamidot, Pennyo, PeterWie, Rbarreira, Scott McNay, Soumyasch, Warren, Wesley crossman, Yukoba, 23 anonymous edits

Windows Driver Kit *Source*: http://en.wikipedia.org/w/index.php?oldid=368519307 *Contributors*: A5b, Andareed, Craigrow, Cwolfsheep, Cynical, Mikeblas, Paul M Wiens, Semperf, Vikizh, Yukoba, 16 anonymous edits

Windows Logo Kit *Source*: http://en.wikipedia.org/w/index.php?oldid=347836041 *Contributors*: Asztal, B-Con, Bachrach44, Craigrow, Djido, Frap, GreyCat, Mr6686, Nandurkumar, Ollie, Soumyasch, TAG.Odessa, Vikizh, Warren, WikiBCS, Yukoba, 4 anonymous edits

X00 *Source*: http://en.wikipedia.org/w/index.php?oldid=354949609 *Contributors*: AVRS, Accounting4Taste, Dawynn, Devotchka, Florida242526, Frap, InsufficientData, JarlaxleArtemis, Kenilworth Terrace, Mattg82, Pcmicro, Pegship, Sarrazip, Wkitty42, 3 anonymous edits

Xpeak *Source*: http://en.wikipedia.org/w/index.php?oldid=367970248 *Contributors*: Bruno.schmidt, Elwikipedista, Fetchcomms

Image Sources, Licenses and Contributors

File:Windows logo.svg *Source*: http://en.wikipedia.org/w/index.php?title=File:Windows_logo.svg *License*: unknown *Contributors*: Blubberboy92, Cflm001, FleetCommand, Koman90, Tyw7, Zzyzx11, 3 anonymous edits

File:Windows 7.png *Source*: http://en.wikipedia.org/w/index.php?title=File:Windows_7.png *License*: unknown *Contributors*: Addihockey10, Althepal, AnOddName, Anakin101, Andyso, AussieLegend, Crazlunatic, Drilnoth, Feinoha, FleetCommand, GSK, Grayshi, James Michael 1, Jan Hofmann, Jjupiter100, Josh the Nerd, LOL, LobStoR, Mephiles602, Ngyikp, OriginalGamer, PhilKnight, RegularBreaker, S0aasdf2sf, SF007, SchuminWeb, Sdrtirs, Sonicdude558, Sotcr, SpaceFlight89, The 888th Avatar, Warren, Wtshymanski, 27 anonymous edits

File:Windows1.0.png *Source*: http://en.wikipedia.org/w/index.php?title=File:Windows1.0.png *License*: unknown *Contributors*: Aiyizo, Diego Moya, FleetCommand, Frogger3140, Gan Luo, Ghettoblaster, Happy Dude, James Michael 1, Kubek15, Michaelkourlas, Neurolysis, Remember the dot, Warren, 3 anonymous edits

File:Windows 3.0 workspace.png *Source*: http://en.wikipedia.org/w/index.php?title=File:Windows_3.0_workspace.png *License*: unknown *Contributors*: Dancraggs, FleetCommand, James Michael 1, Shlomital, Tyomitch, Warren, Yamla, 4 anonymous edits

File:Am windows95 desktop.png *Source*: http://en.wikipedia.org/w/index.php?title=File:Am_windows95_desktop.png *License*: unknown *Contributors*: AlistairMcMillan, Damian Yerrick, Diego Moya, FleetCommand, Ghettoblaster, James Michael 1, Koman90, McLoaf, Shlomital, ViperSnake151, Warren, 4 anonymous edits

File:WindowsCE7.jpg *Source*: http://en.wikipedia.org/w/index.php?title=File:WindowsCE7.jpg *License*: unknown *Contributors*: FleetCommand, Interframe

Image:Windows Family Tree.svg *Source*: http://en.wikipedia.org/w/index.php?title=File:Windows_Family_Tree.svg *License*: Creative Commons Attribution 2.5 *Contributors*: J.int, Linfocito B, NOKIA 3120 classic, 1 anonymous edits

Image:ATI Catalyst Logo.jpg *Source*: http://en.wikipedia.org/w/index.php?title=File:ATI_Catalyst_Logo.jpg *License*: unknown *Contributors*: Colbuckshot, Sfan00 IMG, Silvergoat

Image:ATI Catalyst Control Centre.png *Source*: http://en.wikipedia.org/w/index.php?title=File:ATI_Catalyst_Control_Centre.png *License*: unknown *Contributors*: Fuzzy510, GoddersUK, Mfield, Silvergoat, 1 anonymous edits

File:CUPS.svg *Source*: http://en.wikipedia.org/w/index.php?title=File:CUPS.svg *License*: GNU General Public License *Contributors*: Biktora, Nikola Smolenski, Rtc, Sven

File:Cups simple.svg *Source*: http://en.wikipedia.org/w/index.php?title=File:Cups_simple.svg *License*: Public Domain *Contributors*: User:Sven

File:CUPS-block-diagram.svg *Source*: http://en.wikipedia.org/w/index.php?title=File:CUPS-block-diagram.svg *License*: GNU Free Documentation License *Contributors*: User:Davis080, User:Ta bu shi da yu

File:Cups-1.4-web-interface.png *Source*: http://en.wikipedia.org/w/index.php?title=File:Cups-1.4-web-interface.png *License*: GNU General Public License *Contributors*: Apple Inc.

File:Cups15-web-interface.png *Source*: http://en.wikipedia.org/w/index.php?title=File:Cups15-web-interface.png *License*: GNU General Public License *Contributors*: Gürkan Sengün

File:Gnome2.26-printing-dialogue.png *Source*: http://en.wikipedia.org/w/index.php?title=File:Gnome2.26-printing-dialogue.png *License*: GNU General Public License *Contributors*: RedHat, Inc.

File:KDE Print cups config.png *Source*: http://en.wikipedia.org/w/index.php?title=File:KDE_Print_cups_config.png *License*: GNU General Public License *Contributors*: Original uploader was Ta bu shi da yu at en.wikipedia. Later version(s) were uploaded by KDesk at en.wikipedia.

File:Mandrake-cups-gui.png *Source*: http://en.wikipedia.org/w/index.php?title=File:Mandrake-cups-gui.png *License*: GNU General Public License *Contributors*: Original uploader was Ta bu shi da yu at en.wikipedia

File:Fedora-CUPS-gui.png *Source*: http://en.wikipedia.org/w/index.php?title=File:Fedora-CUPS-gui.png *License*: GNU General Public License *Contributors*: User:IngerAlHaosului

Image:Driver Verifier.png *Source*: http://en.wikipedia.org/w/index.php?title=File:Driver_Verifier.png *License*: unknown *Contributors*: User:Ngyikp

Image:Ndiswrapper.png *Source*: http://en.wikipedia.org/w/index.php?title=File:Ndiswrapper.png *License*: GNU Free Documentation License *Contributors*: Waldo the terrible

Image:Ndisgtk.png *Source*: http://en.wikipedia.org/w/index.php?title=File:Ndisgtk.png *License*: unknown *Contributors*: http://hacktolive.org/

Image:Omega_700px.png *Source*: http://en.wikipedia.org/w/index.php?title=File:Omega_700px.png *License*: Creative Commons Attribution-Sharealike 3.0 *Contributors*: JKos12

Image:ScannerAccessNowEasyLogo.png *Source*: http://en.wikipedia.org/w/index.php?title=File:ScannerAccessNowEasyLogo.png *License*: Creative Commons Attribution-Sharealike 2.5 *Contributors*: Ahunt, Skamphausen

Image:XSane.png *Source*: http://en.wikipedia.org/w/index.php?title=File:XSane.png *License*: GNU General Public License *Contributors*: http://hacktolive.org

File:Simple Scan 1.0.3.png *Source*: http://en.wikipedia.org/w/index.php?title=File:Simple_Scan_1.0.3.png *License*: GNU General Public License *Contributors*: Robert Ancell

Image:Microsoft UAA Logo.png *Source*: http://en.wikipedia.org/w/index.php?title=File:Microsoft_UAA_Logo.png *License*: unknown *Contributors*: CyberSkull, MECU, Warren, 1 anonymous edits

License

\MBLE

pose of this License is to make a manual, textbook, or ıctional and useful document "free" in the sense of : to assure everyone the effective freedom to copy and ute it, with or without modifying it, either commercially or mercially. Secondarily, this License preserves for the nd publisher a way to get credit for their work, while not nsidered responsible for modifications made by others. ense is a kind of "copyleft", which means that derivative the document must themselves be free in the same complements the GNU General Public License, which is ft license designed for free software. We have designed nse in order to use it for manuals for free software, free software needs free documentation: a free program ome with manuals providing the same freedoms that the does. But this License is not limited to software manuals; used for any textual work, regardless of subject matter ıer it is published as a printed book. We recommend this principally for works whose purpose is instruction or e.

.ICABILITY AND DEFINITIONS

ense applies to any manual or ot her work, in any , that contains a notice placed by the copyright holder can be distributed under the terms of this License. Such grants a world -wide, royalty -free license, unlimited in , to use that work under the conditio ns stated herein. The ent", below, refers to any such manual or work. Any of the public is a licensee, and is addressed as "you". ept the license if you copy, modify or distribute the work requiring permission under copyright l aw. A "Modified of the Document means any work containing the nt or a portion of it, either copied verbatim, or with tions and/or translated into another language. A lary Section" is a named appendix or a front -matter o f the Document that deals exclusively with the ship of the publishers or authors of the Document to the nt's overall subject (or to related matters) and contains that could fall directly within that overall subject. (Thus, if ıment is in part a textbook of mathematics, a Secondary may not explain any mathematics.) The relationship could tter of historical connection with the subject or with matters, or of legal, commercial, philosophical, ethical or position regarding them. The "Invariant Sections" are Secondary Sections whose titles are designated, as being Invariant Sections, in the notice that says that the nt is released under this License. If a section does not fit ve definition of Secondary then it is not allowed to be ted as Invariant. The Document may contain zero t Sections. If the Document does not identify any Invariant s then there are none. The "Cover Texts" are certain short s of text that are listed, as Front -Cover Texts or Back - 'exts, in the notice that says that the Document is d under this License. A Front -Cover Text may be at most , and a Back -Cover Text may be at most 25 words. A arent" copy of the Document means a machine -readable presented in a format whose specification is available to eral public, that is suitable for revising the document orwardly with generic text editors or (for images ed of pixels) generic p aint programs or (for drawings) idely available drawing editor, and that is suitable for input ormatters or for automatic translation to a variety of suitable for input to text formatters. A copy made in an e Transparent file format whose markup, or absence of has been arranged to thwart or discourage subsequent tion by readers is not Transparent. An image format is ısparent if used for any substantial amount of text. A copy ot "Transparent" is called "Opaque". Examples of suitable for Transparent copies include plain ASCII without , Texinfo input format, LaTeX input format, SGML or XML publicly available DTD, and standard -conforming simple PostScript or PDF designed f or human modification. es of transparent image formats include PNG, XCF and paque formats include proprietary formats that can be d edited only by proprietary word processors, SGML or which the DTD and/or processing tools are not generally e, and the machine -generated HTML, PostScript or PDF d by some word processors for output purposes only. The age" means, for a printed book, the title page itself, plus lowing pages as are needed to hold, legibly, the material ense requires to appear in the title page. For works in which do not have any title page as such, "Title Page" the text near the most prominent appearance of the work's ceding the beginning of the body of the te xt. A section d XYZ" means a named subunit of the Document whose er is precisely XYZ or contains XYZ in parentheses g text that translates XYZ in another language. (Here XYZ for a specific section name mentioned below, such as wledgements", "Dedications", "Endorsements", or ".) To "Preserve the Title" of such a section when you the Document means that it remains a section "Entitled cording to this definition. The Document may include ty Disc laimers next to the notice which states that this applies to the Document. These Warranty Disclaimers sidered to be included by reference in this License, but regards disclaiming warranties: any other implication that arranty Disclaimers may have is void and has no effect neaning of this License.

BATIM COPYING

ay copy and distribute the Document in any medium, ommercially or noncommercially, provided that this , the copyright notices, and the license notice saying this License applies to the Document are reproduced in all copies, and that you add no other conditions whatsoever to those of this License. You may not use technical measures to obstruct or control the reading or further copying of t he copies you make or distribute. However, you may accept compensation in exchange for copies. If you distribute a large enough number of copies you must also follow the conditions in section 3. You may also lend copies, under the same conditions stated ab ove, and you may publicly display copies.

3. COPYING IN QUANTITY

If you publish printed copies (or copies in media that commonly have printed covers) of the Document, numbering more than 100, and the Document's license notice requires Cover Texts, you must enclose the copies in covers that carry, clearly and legibly, all these Cover Texts: Front -Cover Texts on the front cover, and Back-Cover Texts on the back cover. Both covers must also clearly and legibly identify you as the publisher of these copies. The front cover must present the full title with all words of the title equally prominent and visible. You may add other material on the covers in addition. Copying with changes limited to the covers, as long as they preserve the title of the Document and s atisfy these conditions, can be treated as verbatim copying in other respects. If the required texts for either cover are too voluminous to fit legibly, you should put the first ones listed (as many as fit reasonably) on the actual cover, and continue the rest onto adjacent pages. If you publish or distribute Opaque copies of the Document numbering more than 100, you must either include a machine-readable Transparent copy along with each Opaque copy, or state in or with each Opaque copy a computer -network location from which the general network -using public has access to download using public -standard network protocols a complete Transparent copy of the Document, free of added material. If you use the latter option, you must take reasonably prudent steps, when you begin distribution of Opaque copies in quantity, to ensure that this Transparent copy will remain thus accessible at the stated location until at least one year after the last time you distribute an Opaque copy (directly or through your agents or retailers) of that edition to the public. It is requested, but not required, that you contact the authors of the Document well before redistributing any large number of copies, to give them a chance to provide you with an updated version of the Document.

4. MODIFICATIONS

You may copy and distribute a Modified Version of the Document under the conditions of sections 2 and 3 above, provided that you release the Modified Version under precisely this License, with the Modified Version filling the role of the Do cument, thus licensing distribution and modification of the Modified Version to whoever possesses a copy of it. In addition, you must do these things in the Modified Version: A. Use in the Title Page (and on the covers, if any) a title distinct from that o f the Document, and from those of previous versions (which should, if there were any, be listed in the History section of the Document). You may use the same title as a previous version if the original publisher of that version gives permission. B. List on the Title Page, as authors, one or more persons or entities responsible for authorship of the modifications in the Modified Version, together with at least five of the principal authors of the Document (all of its principal authors, if it has fewer than f ive), unless they release you from this requirement. C. State on the Title page the name of the publisher of the Modified Version, as the publisher. D. Preserve all the copyright notices of the Document. E. Add an appropriate copyright notice for your modi fications adjacent to the other copyright notices. F. Include, immediately after the copyright notices, a license notice giving the public permission to use the Modified Version under the terms of this License, in the form shown in the Addendum below. G. Preserve in that license notice the full lists of Invariant Sections and required Cover Texts given in the Document's license notice. H. Include an unaltered copy of this License. I. Preserve the section Entitled "History", Preserve its Title, and add to it an item stating at least the title, year, new authors, and publisher of the Modified Version as given on the Title Page. If there is no section Entitled "History" in the Document, create one stating the title, year, authors, and publisher of the Document as given on its Title Page, then add an item describing the Modified Version as stated in the previous sentence. J. Preserve the network location, if any, given in the Document for public access to a Transparent copy of the Document, and likewise the netwo rk locations given in the Document for previous versions it was based on. These may be placed in the "History" section. You may omit a network location for a work that was published at least four years before the Document itself, or if the original publish er of the version it refers to gives permission. K. For any section Entitled "Acknowledgements" or "Dedications", Preserve the Title of the section, and preserve in the section all the substance and tone of each of the contributor acknowledgements and/or d edications given therein. L. Preserve all the Invariant Sections of the Document, unaltered in their text and in their titles. Section numbers or the equivalent are not considered part of the section titles. M. Delete any section Entitled "Endorsements". S uch a section may not be included in the Modified Version. N. Do not retitle any existing section to be Entitled "Endorsements" or to conflict in title with any Invariant Section. O. Preserve any Warranty Disclaimers. If the Modified Version includes new f ront-matter sections or appendices that qualify as Secondary Sections and contain no material copied from the Document, you may at your option designate some or all of these sections as invariant. To do this, add their titles to the list of Invariant Secti ons in the Modified Version's license notice. These titles must be distinct from any other section titles. You may add a section Entitled "Endorsements", provided it contains nothing but endorsements of your Modified Version by various parties --for example , statements of peer review or that the text has been approved by an organization as the authoritative definition of a standard. You may add a passage of up to five words as a Front -Cover Text, and a passage of up to 25 words as a Back -Cover Text, to the end of the list of Cover Texts in the Modified Version. Only one passage of Front-Cover Text and one of Back -Cover Text may be added by (or through arrangements made by) any one entity. If the Document already includes a cover text for the same cover, previously added by you or by arrangement made by the same entity you are acting on behalf of, you may not add another; but you may replace the old one, on explicit permission from the previous publisher that added the old one. The author(s) and publisher(s) of the Document do not by this License give permission to use their names for publicity for or to assert or imply endorsement of any Modified Version.

5. COMBINING DOCUMENTS

You may combine the Document with other documents released under this License, under the terms defined in section 4 above for modified versions, provided that you include in the combination all of the Invariant Sections of all of the original documents, unmodified, and list them all as Invariant Sections of your combined work in its lic ense notice, and that you preserve all their Warranty Disclaimers. The combined work need only contain one copy of this License, and multiple identical Invariant Sections may be replaced with a single copy. If there are multiple Invariant Sections with the same name but different contents, make the title of each such section unique by adding at the end of it, in parentheses, the name of the original author or publisher of that section if known, or else a unique number. Make the same adjustment to the sectio n titles in the list of Invariant Sections in the license notice of the combined work. In the combination, you must combine any sections Entitled "History" in the various original documents, forming one section Entitled "History"; likewise combine any sect ions Entitled "Acknowledgements", and any sections Entitled "Dedications". You must delete all sections Entitled "Endorsements".

6. COLLECTIONS OF DOCUMENTS

You may make a collection consisting of the Document and other documents released under this Lice nse, and replace the individual copies of this License in the various documents with a single copy that is included in the collection, provided that you follow the rules of this License for verbatim copying of each of the documents in all other respects. Y ou may extract a single document from such a collection, and distribute it individually under this License, provided you insert a copy of this License into the extracted document, and follow this License in all other respects regarding verbatim copying of that document.

7. AGGREGATION WITH INDEPENDENT WORKS

A compilation of the Document or its derivatives with other separate and independent documents or works, in or on a volume of a storage or distribution medium, is called an "aggregate" if the copyright resulting from the compilation is not used to limit the legal rights of the compilation's users beyond what the individual works permit. When the Document is included in an aggregate, this License does not apply to the other works in the aggregate which are not themselves derivative works of the Document. If the Cover Text requirement of section 3 is applicable to these copies of the Document, then if the Document is less than one half of the entire aggregate, the Document's Cover Texts may be placed on covers that bracket the Document within the aggregate, or the electronic equivalent of covers if the Document is in electronic form. Otherwise they must appear on printed covers that bracket the whole aggregate.

8. TRANSLATION

Translation is considered a k ind of modification, so you may distribute translations of the Document under the terms of section 4. Replacing Invariant Sections with translations requires special permission from their copyright holders, but you may include translations of some or all I nvariant Sections in addition to the original versions of these Invariant Sections. You may include a translation of this License, and all the license notices in the Document, and any Warranty Disclaimers, provided that you also include the original Englis h version of this License and the original versions of those notices and disclaimers. In case of a disagreement between the translation and the original version of this License or a notice or disclaimer, the original version will prevail. If a section in t he Document is Entitled "Acknowledgements", "Dedications", or "History", the requirement (section 4) to Preserve its Title (section 1) will typically require changing the actual title.

9. TERMINATION

You may not copy, modify, sublicense, or distribute th e Document except as expressly provided for under this License. Any other attempt to copy, modify, sublicense or distribute the Document is void, and will automatically terminate your rights under this License. However, parties who have received copies, or rights, from you under this License will not have their licenses terminated so long as such parties remain in full compliance.

10. FUTURE REVISIONS OF THIS LICENSE

The Free Software Foundation may publish new, revised versions of the GNU Free Documentat ion License from time to time. Such new versions will be similar in spirit to the present version, but may differ in detail to address new problems or concerns. See http://www.gnu.org/copyleft/. Each version of the License is given a distinguishing version number. If the Document specifies that a particular numbered version of this License "or any later version" applies to it, you have the option of following the terms and conditions either of that specified version or of any later version that has been pub lished (not as a draft) by the Free Software Foundation. If the Document does not specify a version number of this License, you may choose any version ever published (not as a draft) by the Free Software Foundation. ADDENDUM: How to use this License for yo ur documents To use this License in a document you have written, include a copy of the License in the document and put the following copyright and license notices just after the title page: Copyright (c) YEAR YOUR NAME. Permission is granted to copy, distr ibute and/or modify this document under the terms of the GNU Free Documentation License, Version 1.2 or any later version published by the Free Software Foundation; with no Invariant Sections, no Front -Cover Texts, and no Back-Cover Texts. A copy of the li cense is included in the section entitled "GNU Free Documentation License". If you have Invariant Sections, Front -Cover Texts and Back -Cover Texts, replace the "with...Texts." line with this: with the Invariant Sections being LIST THEIR TITLES, with the Fr ont-Cover Texts being LIST, and with the Back -Cover Texts being LIST. If you have Invariant Sections without Cover Texts, or some other combination of the three, merge those two alternatives to suit the situation. If your document contains nontrivial examp les of program code, we recommend releasing these examples in parallel under your choice of free software license, such as the GNU General Public License, to permit their use in free software.

CPSIA information can be obtained at www.ICGtesting.com
Printed in the USA
LVOW041555220312

274341LV00004B/70/P

9 786132 227232